Leadership in Health Care

Leadership is a hugely important topic especially when considered in the context of the challenges that European health care systems are facing. Rooted in a practising chief executive's own experience and primary research, *Leadership in Health Care* is a challenging and accessible new text that sheds new light on the complex issue of leadership in health care.

Presenting new research alongside a practical model for developing personal leadership in health care, this text bridges the gulf between academia and practice, making it essential reading for students of health management and all those involved in health care management.

Neil Goodwin is both a health care chief executive and a leadership academic. He is Chief Executive of the Greater Manchester Strategic Health Authority, the largest strategic body in the English National Health Service. He is also Visiting Professor in Leadership Studies at Manchester Business School and a visiting fellow at Durham University.

ROUTLEDGE HEALTH MANAGEMENT SERIES

Edited by Marc Berg, Robbert Huijsman, David Hunter, John Øvretveit

Routledge Health Management is one of the first series of its kind, filling the need for a comprehensive and balanced series of textbooks on core management topics specifically oriented towards the health care field. In almost all Western countries, health care is seen to be in a state of radical reorientation. Each title in this series will focus on a core topic within health care management, and will concentrate explicitly on the knowledge and insights required to meet the challenges of being a health care manager. With a strong international orientation, each book draws heavily on case examples and vignettes to illustrate the theories at play. A genuinely groundbreaking new series in a much-needed area, this series has been put together by an international collection of expert editors and teachers.

Health Information Management
Integrating information technology in health care work
Marc Berg with others

Health Operations Management
Patient flow logistics in health care
Jan Vissers and Roger Beech

Leadership in Health Care
A European perspective
Neil Goodwin

Performance Management in Health Care
Improving patient outcomes, an integrated approach
Jan Walburg, Helen Bevan, John Wilderspin and Karin Lemmens

Leadership in Health Care

A European perspective

Neil Goodwin

Routledge
Taylor & Francis Group

LONDON AND NEW YORK

First published 2006
by Routledge
2 Park Square, Milton Park, Abingdon, Oxon OX14 4RN

Simultaneously published in the USA and Canada
by Routledge
270 Madison Ave, New York, NY 10016

Routledge is an imprint of the Taylor & Francis Group

© 2006 Neil Goodwin

Typeset in Perpetua and Bell Gothic by
Florence Production Ltd, Stoodleigh, Devon
Printed and bound in Great Britain by
MPG Books Ltd, Bodmin

British Library Cataloguing in Publication Data
A catalogue record for this book is available from the British Library

Library of Congress Cataloging in Publication Data
A catalog record for this book has been requested

ISBN10: 0–415–34327–5 (hbk)
ISBN10: 0–415–34328–3 (pbk)

ISBN13: 9–78–0–415–34327–5 (hbk)
ISBN13: 9–78–0–415–34328–2 (pbk)

For Matthew and Owen

Contents

Illustrations

TABLES

FIGURES

Acknowledgements

I am grateful to friends and colleagues across Europe and at home for their guidance, support and constructive criticism. I am especially grateful to David Hunter, Tom van der Grinton, Philip Berman, Mats Larson, Jari Vouri, Barrie Fisher and Rachel Mann. Their comments and suggestions have been invaluable.

Combining production of this book with my full-time job in the English NHS has been a considerable personal challenge. I could not have continued with either without the help of Carole Ogden, who typed my early drafts of chapters superlatively, and Joanne Downey, who managed my time without my knowing it.

Finally, I am grateful for the support of my partner, Chris Hannah. As a successful health care leader in her own right she suggested a number of positive changes to the drafts, as well as bearing the intrusion of my writing with typical good humour.

Introduction

This book is about three things: leadership, health care and Europe. Each is changing fast and all are linked because of that. We cannot change health care services, organisations and systems without leadership. We cannot practice leadership of health care across the countries of Europe without considering the development and impact of the European Union, which is now the largest politically and economically integrated transnational bloc in the world. In addition, because of the increasing links between leadership, health and Europe, a discussion about all three is long overdue, which is why this is the first book devoted to the leadership of health care across the countries of Europe. The book is also timely given the increasing political and public interest in the growing influence of the European Union.

The approach to leadership presented in this book is based on the view that it is distinctly different from management and strongly context driven. The context and challenges for health and health care across Europe are changing rapidly and in many cases are converging. Although no European countries are alike when it comes to health care and the systems are different, each country is facing the same fundamental challenges for three reasons (Salfeld and Vaagan 2004). First, although differences between the funding systems of European countries have become less significant as a result of health service reforms in recent years, health care spending is increasing significantly faster than gross domestic product (GDP). This is not good news and when coupled with high employment that exists in some countries, for example Germany is currently ten per cent, maintaining levels of taxation and social insurance is unlikely to be sustainable by governments. Second, there are significant quality differences between countries, for example mortality rates for breast cancer are 37 per cent in Italy compared to 24 per cent in Sweden. Third, patients are beginning to behave as consumers and demand more information about, and improved access to, health care services. If necessary they also are prepared to travel to different countries for faster access to treatment. The European Court of Justice has ruled that it is reasonable for patients to receive treatment without undue delay, and for them to be reimbursed by their own country under existing treaty provisions governing the free movement of goods and services. To tackle these challenges numerous solutions are being tested under the broad heading of reform and since publication of the World Health Report (WHO 2000), comparisons of health system performance are now very much on the international policy agenda (Nolte and McKee 2003).

Population health is also a major challenge for the countries of Europe. The health challenges of the separate countries are beginning to converge and are the result of demographic, lifestyle and environmental changes. People are living longer and new pharmacological developments appear every year along with other developments in life support for patients. Population health is generating similar challenges, for example it is estimated that between 20 and 30 per cent of adults in Europe are overweight because of poor diet and lack of physical activity. Cardiovascular disease is now responsible for 40 per cent of all deaths across Europe. Although health and health care may be viewed as an economic burden it is also an asset in terms of employment and economic regeneration. Consequently, in the context of the relationship between health and overall socio-economic development it is difficult to imagine the health care industry not being at the centre of the movement to achieve a more integrated Europe.

The word leadership is found in every language and is almost as old as civilisation itself. Our historical interest in leadership shows no sign of waning. Bass's (1990) revised edition of Stogdill's Handbook of Leadership lists thousands of references to leadership studies. Between 1974 and 1990 the number of references in the handbook increased by several thousand while hundreds of new articles on leadership are published in academic journals every year. At the last count there were over 400 definitions of leadership. Questions about leadership never stop, which is probably a reflection of the fact that answers are not easily found. Are leaders born or made? Can we learn the skills that leaders employ to achieve success? What is the difference between leadership and management; and what impact, if any, do the political and organisational environments within which we work have on the development of leaders? How important is the culture of our employing organisations or the people we work with on our ability to pursue leadership? What is the relationship between leadership and other areas of research and human behaviour such as power and trust? How should leaders deal with difficult situations, difficult people and cope with personal failure? For leaders in health care, what is the impact of national governmental and international health and social care policies? Are there special considerations when thinking about leading clinical professionals and teams?

I have always been struck when reading leadership books that they are either fundamentally practical or else highly academic but rarely are the two approaches combined in a single publication. In many ways this reflects the dichotomy that exists when writing about leadership. We often try to explain the phenomenon theoretically or we describe it practically but rarely do we discuss the two together. It is no wonder that academics struggle to produce a coherent view of leadership for the benefit of both students of leadership and its practitioners. This book has that ambitious aim and therefore its target readership is these two groups – students of management and leadership, and practising health care managers across the countries of Europe.

In the light of the above, making sense of the copious leadership and related literature is a challenge for most busy health care leaders whether in general or clinical management. Add to that the contextual and demographic challenges of health and health care across Europe and the role of the leader of an organisation, service or network becomes positively daunting. To help the busy reader to focus on the essentials of leadership the book is structured as follows:

- Chapters 1–3 address the 'what' of leadership. Chapters 1 and 2 present an overview of the topic including the main leadership styles and how they apply in practice.
- Chapter 3 explores the converging context of health and health care in European countries as it affects the leaders of today and tomorrow. Chapters 1–3 also cover public sector management research as well as references to recent research in the health care sector.
- Chapters 4 and 5 address the 'how' of leadership. They follow the conclusions of Chapter 3, namely that health care leadership in Europe is increasingly about leading through networks, partnership and collaboration. This is discussed in Chapter 4; and in order to create sustainable networks and networking, which are based on interpersonal relationships, Chapter 5 discusses the academic and practical basis for that, namely emotional intelligence with its emphasis on the development of interpersonal skills and self-awareness.
- To illustrate how the academic literature and the practical reality of health care leadership are linked together, Chapter 6 presents the results of qualitative research on how chief executives implemented real time change to their local health care systems. The chapter concludes with a proposed model for health care leadership.

■ To conclude, Chapter 7 focuses on the importance of understanding failure, which is a normal part of development for everyone, and its links to the development of personal leadership skills.

Finally, because the book's main aim is to bridge the gulf between the academic and the practical, each chapter concludes with a bibliography for those wishing to read more extensively and a series of discussion questions. These questions aim to help the reader think through the issues and relate the key learning from the chapter to his or her own day-to-day reality in European health care. Neither the bibliography nor the discussion questions are essential but if pursued they will enrich the reader's personal development, and understanding and enjoyment of leadership and its related fields.

BIBLIOGRAPHY AND FURTHER READING

Bass B.M. (1990) *Bass and Stogdill's Handbook of Leadership Theory, Research and Managerial Applications*. New York: The Free Press.

Nolte E. and McKee M. (2003) Population health in Europe: how much is attributable to health care? *Euro Observer* 5(4): 1–3.

Salfeld R. and Vaagan M. (2004) The road to reform in Europe. *Health Europe. Management know-how for the health care industry* 3, March: 14–29.

World Health Organization (2000) *The World Health Report. Health Systems Performance: improving performance.* Geneva: WHO.

Chapter 1

Introducing leadership

KEY POINTS OF THIS CHAPTER

- Research on leadership has been prolific but it is resistant to definition.
- Leadership and management are different but they are not mutually exclusive.
- Leadership is essentially a relationship-based activity.
- Context, vision, passion and follower engagement are important components of leadership.
- Overall leadership effectiveness is not influenced by gender.
- There are links between leadership and other literature such as power and trust.
- There are numerous myths about leadership.

KEY TERMS

- Leadership
- Management
- Vision
- Context
- Gender
- Social relations

WHAT ARE LEADERSHIP AND MANAGEMENT?

Definitions of leadership are too numerous to list and there are almost as many definitions as there are writers on the subject. To take a typical definition:

> Leadership exists when someone (the leader) exercises influence over others (the followers) in their group or organisation. Their influence may be wide-ranging or narrowly focused but within formal organisations they particularly emphasise: values that are espoused; directions in which future developments are guided; and the manner in which everyday tasks are accomplished.
>
> (Dawson 1996)

There are three critical points from this definition. First, leadership is not a characteristic of any one individual working in isolation. Leadership is played out between leaders and followers, without whom leadership cannot exist. Second, there can be numerous leaders in one organisation, each leading on different issues. And third, leadership is not always synonymous with hierarchical position. Leaders can be found at different levels and in different departments, services or networks across an organisation. At this point the reader should note that throughout the book leadership is most frequently referred to in the context of the organisation but it is equally applicable to other contexts such as a service or department, a clinical or inter-organisational network, and a health care or inter-agency system. In addition, Chapter 4 on networks, partnerships and collaboration discusses specific aspects of leading and working across service, departmental and organisational boundaries.

MANAGEMENT AND LEADERSHIP

A frequently asked question is, what is the difference between management and leadership? In general, although most commentators would agree that there are differences, they are unlikely to agree on the extent of the differences. Rost (1993) identifies four substantive differences between the two (see Table 1.1).

The first three differences are clear enough but the remaining difference appears less distinctive and therefore may be more difficult to use. Mutual purposes are best described as common purposes developed over time as followers and leaders interact in a non-coercive or non-hierarchical relationship about the changes they support. There is nothing in the definition of management about mutual purposes, so when that begins to happen between

Table 1.1 *Distinguishing leadership from management*

Leadership	Management
■ Influence relationship	■ Authority relationship
■ Leaders and followers	■ Managers and subordinates
■ Intend real changes	■ Produce and sell goods and/or services
■ Intended changes reflect mutual purposes	■ Goods/services result from coordinated activities

people, it is leadership that is emerging. Leaders and followers are constantly in the process of developing mutual purposes and their commitment to that purpose makes the leadership relationship different from the management relationship. Rost's definition of leadership, with its emphasis on mutual purposes, is one of the few definitions that takes the role of followers in leadership into account.

Management is a largely a twentieth-century phenomenon that emerged with the creation of large manufacturing organisations, for example car production. The aim of management is to cope with organisational complexity and provide stability. It is essentially concerned with the implementation of decisions. There are always four key processes at the heart of virtually all descriptions of management: planning, budgeting, organising and controlling. In the hierarchical relationships that continue to exist within many organisations, managers use authority based on their formal position by working in a single and top-down way. In contrast, leaders attempt to influence other people in a number of different directions often beyond their own department or service and increasingly today, beyond their organisation's boundary to other organisations.

Management is different from leadership in that it is more formal and scientific with a set of explicit analytical and decision-making tools and techniques based on rational reasoning that are designed to be used in similar ways across a wide range of situations. Managers are concerned with keeping the system turning over and although they will often propose change it will be mainly by changing structures and reorganising work processes. Short-term success can result but with little lasting beneficial effect. From another perspective, management can be viewed as an attribution made to explain performance, while leadership is viewed as a social construction that serves to rationalise and reinforce existing patterns of social relations (Bresnen 1995). This view, which is based on discussion with practising managers, argues that although attribution-based approaches are valuable they largely ignore the impact of broader social relations. Although the practising managers involved in the research offered some support for the notion that leadership embodies prevailing assumptions about the distribution of power, authority and control, this rested uneasily with their personal, experiential and phenomenological differences that they use to construct their own theories and explanations of leadership. In other words, there is a gulf between those who study leadership and those who practise it. There has been only ad hoc development of schools of leadership and although the UK public sector has a number of separate leadership centres, for example in health and education, there is not a leadership school for the public sector as a whole. This gulf between academics and managers can make it difficult to frame and understand what makes sense for those who want not only to study leadership but also to put the concept to work.

Managers will tend to view work as an enabling tool, helping processes along by assessing potential opposition and controversy and reducing tensions when they arise by seeking compromise solutions. Not surprisingly, managerial tactics are based on transactions including negotiation and bargaining along with the use of rewards, punishments or other forms of coercion. In contrast, leaders work in the opposite direction by not limiting choices but developing fresh approaches to long-standing problems. What this means is that managers, rather than leaders, relate to people according to the role they play in a sequence of events or in production and decision-making processes; while leaders, who are more concerned with ideas, relate in more intuitive and empathetic ways. In other words, they view people from an emotional perspective and they see them as human beings with distinct and individual personalities.

Others reflect these views. Wheatley (1999) reminds us that one quality particular to human beings is the need to know 'why'; to understand and ascribe meaning to events and change. When people can reflect on their experiences and develop an interpretation of an event then they are more able to endure major change. Research in UK health systems has confirmed that successfully tackling issues or events that are seen as important to local players is an almost necessary precursor to addressing major, externally driven change, such as that from national government (Goodwin 2002). There is also evidence of UK NHS nurse leaders performing an interpretation and translation role in order to bridge the divide between the policy context and practice (Antrobus and Kitson 1999). The ability to make sense of the wider working context, for example the impact of new government policy, and to interpret and describe the likely impact within the local working context, is a powerful leadership skill.

There are some who see leadership as an integral part of the manager's role, arguing that while formal authority gives the manager power, it is leadership, exercised through non-coercive, interpersonal relationships, that determines in large part how much of it is used (Mintzberg 1989). The importance of inter-personal relationships in leadership is underscored by 'soft' systems thinking (Checkland 1985). The term 'soft' is used because of its support for the impor-tance of maintaining relationships as opposed to 'hard' systems thinking with its emphasis on goal-seeking found in the management science of the 1950s and 1960s. This is a social constructional approach, which reflects the view that lead-ership is rarely a one-way process and is strongly associated with other organ-isational processes of power, communication and decision-making. In other words, leadership is seen when one or more people succeed in framing and defining the reality of others and these people emerge as leaders because their framing of reality provides a viable basis for action. Again, it is about explaining 'why' and the impact of wider context on individuals and organisations. And for most large organisations and industrial sectors, including health care, the operating and political context is now more complex than ever before.

Finally, although management and leadership can be very different they are not mutually exclusive; for example, managers' plans do not have to include a vision and budgets do not necessarily have strategies (Kotter 1990). In relatively stable working environments, limited leadership coupled with strong manage-ment would work well but in times of major change or chaos, strong leader-ship with some limited management may be what is required. In summary, leadership is essentially concerned with pursuing change via the development of influential and empathetic interpersonal relationships; and the process that leaders will go through to achieve that is essentially twofold:

- first, creating an agenda for change using a strong vision;
- second, building a strong implementation network to get things done through other people.

CONTEXT

Although there is a strong theme in the literature supporting the view that leadership is the critical factor in determining organisational success or failure, this underplays the significant environmental, macro-economic, political and business influences that potentially impact on organisational performance. It is important to note that there has been much more research on the consequences of leader behaviour than on its determinants such as the impact of external forces on the effects of leadership (Lieberson and O'Connor 1972; Yukl 1994). This is probably because of the widespread bias to perceive leaders as players who shape events rather than being shaped by them. Strong advocates of leadership argue that leadership is the pivotal force behind successful organ-isations because it provides vision and the mobilisation of people to achieve change. The alternative view is reflected by resource dependency, which asserts that organisational performance depends primarily on factors such as economic conditions, government policies and technological change (Pfeffer 1982). Unfortunately, only a few theories have been developed to explain how the context in which leaders operate actually influences behaviour.

Two questions can be asked about the relationship between leadership and organisational performance (Thomas 1988). First, to what extent do leader differences account for performance variations within organisations over time? Second, to what extent do leader differences account for the total variation displayed by a whole set of organisations, which includes both intra- and inter-organisational variance, in comparison with that accounted for by contextual variables? Lieberson and O'Connor (ibid.) argue that leadership influence is a product of the internal and external constraints on the leader and his or her relative ability. Consequently, if differences cannot be seen when there is a change of leader then does it matter who occupies the position or how they behave? This is often referred to as the ambiguity of leadership (Pfeffer 1997). Leaders in high-level positions, such as chief executives and senior executives actually have unilateral control over fewer resources and policies than might be assumed. Many decisions, such as investment proposals or major organisational change require the support and approval of other senior managers, often the board of directors or sometimes other organisations and external stakeholders. What this means is that organisations and the people within them will often constrain the behaviour of their leaders and consequently, the observed effects of leaders on organisational outcomes may actually be small.

Another way of looking at this is from the work of Kakabadse and Kakabadse (1999), who argue that the alternate pursuit of vertical and horizontal synergy strategies in an organisation can rapidly create a leadership gap. Vertical syner-gies are concerned with economics, cost, structures of organisations and over-heads. They are the components requiring constant attention and adjustment in order for the organisation to operate efficiently. Thus, pursuing a vertical synergy strategy focuses on sustaining competitive advantage on price and cost. In contrast, horizontal synergies are concerned with issues of quality, being responsive to market needs, providing a service and being sympathetic to the needs of consumers, other organisations perhaps, and to staff and management internally. To pursue horizontal synergies requires a consultative management style including teamwork, open communication and an attitude of sharing and cooperation. For organisational leaders facing these vertical and horizontal challenges a paradox may be generated: how can costs be controlled at the same time as promoting an internal environment of openness, trust and cooperation? Is it possible to lead effectively but separately for vertical and horizontal synergy strategies? The result may be a leadership gap filled by strife, division, tension and fundamental differences of view concerning the future, with individuals having no sense of responsibility for their leadership role.

Wisdom and maturity are also important characteristics for the more effective leaders. In their book, *Geeks and Geezers*, Bennis and Thomas (2002) confirm that among leaders there is an enormous variance in IQ, birth order, family wealth, family stability, level of education, ethnicity, race and gender. Although these factors cannot be dismissed entirely when assessing leaders, it is adaptive capacity that is the single quality that determines success. Adaptive capacity includes critical skills such as the ability to understand context and to recognise and seize opportunities. It is the essential competence of leaders. It is the ability to view a challenge or crisis laterally and see a number of possible unconventional solutions. In a study of leadership development in 30 public and private sector organisations Alimo-Metcalfe and Lawler (2001) found evidence of a contextual model of leadership, by which is meant that leadership is contingent on factors such as culture and interpersonal working. Also, Pettigrew *et al.* (1994) identifies cooperative inter-organisational networks as one of eight key factors for successful change in the UK NHS. While the importance of context in leadership studies continues to be debated, what is probably true is that the leader, at any level within an organisation, is potentially the biggest influence on their immediate operating environment. This is because people working in a formal hierarchy particularly feel their main identity is with their department or service rather than with the whole organisation. Consequently, most people are often only dimly aware of wider contextual issues both within and beyond their organisation.

In the light of these differences of view about the added value of leadership, it is not surprising that the question is asked whether leadership matters at all because of the degree that leaders can actually influence organisational performance. Consequently, we should not be surprised to hear it argued that leadership is much less important than is believed. It is likely that the answer lies between those supporting the contextual view and those strongly supporting the concept of leadership. However, strong evidence for either is difficult to establish because of the challenge of gaining access to observe top management in action in organisations or in carrying out controlled investigations of organisations. This is because it is impracticable for organisational research to be undertaken in controlled, laboratory conditions. What we need to understand about context is that it is important to leaders because they rely extensively on their ability to read situations. Good leaders sense an environment, absorbing and interpreting soft data without having it spelt out for them. Is this a natural instinct or can it be learned? It is probably both and it is certainly true that some individuals seem to have a natural intuitive ability to read situations. On the other hand, many managers have clearly improved their ability in that area through improving their emotional intelligence and systematic training in interpersonal skills. Emotional intelligence is discussed further in Chapter 5.

VISION AND PASSION

Vision

Vision is the essence of leadership and it is often synonymous with the terms 'mission' and 'strategic direction'. It is a prerequisite to providing inspiration and momentum. This is important in leadership because people are not led by paper policies, strategies and quantitative analysis. People actually do business with other people. Vision is an agreement about future direction. It is a positive image of what an organisation or service could become and the path towards that aim. Determining direction and purpose is of paramount importance for the leader; it is the basis on which the leader acts and seeks to secure followers. Consequently, the content of a vision is crucial in determining whether its aims will be achieved.

The research in this area is limited and since leadership is a people process the research has focused primarily on entrepreneurs, for example Steven Jobs of Apple Computers, Anita Roddick of The Body Shop, Jack Welch of General Electric, Jan Carlson of Scandinavian Airways and Richard Branson of Virgin. These entrepreneurial individuals have been or are very charismatic leaders operating in successful industries and, therefore, it is debatable whether they are truly representative. What is known from the research is that a leader's vision has to evolve within the context or environment of the organisation or service. In addition, the vision of the charismatic leader must be empathetic to, and reflect the shared concern of, followers and supporters. For example, the success of the UK's environmentally sensitive The Body Shop cannot be separated from the growth of the Green movement across Western Europe in the 1980s. Similarly, the success of Richard Branson's Virgin Group reflects consumer desire for change across Europe and the US in both retail and low-cost transport, an approach that has now been replicated by many competitors.

One of the most important roles of a leader is to make the vision meaningful largely through language, actions and stories. Storytelling can be very powerful in leadership: as in life generally, people respond to images and stories in their work. What effective leaders do is to provide a framework of understanding so that their followers know what they are doing and why. Implementing vision requires high levels of follower commitment and performance, instilling in followers the value, beliefs and behaviours necessary for the vision's realisation, and devising and executing strategic initiatives that further the vision within the organisation and beyond. When it is communicated clearly, vision seems simple. Consider Henry Ford's *I will build a motor car for the great multitude*; Federal Express founder Fred Smith's *To deliver all packages within 24 hours*; or more simply, Walt Disney's *To make people happy*; and shorter still, Honda's *Destroy Yamaha!* But leaders can make mistakes in defining their vision of where they and their followers should go. To get it right leaders need to remember two things. First, vision is not to be confused with mission. Vision is the long-term aspiration of the business or organisation or service, for example achieving the best reputation or being the most reliable; while mission is a higher purpose focusing on the broader impact on society. To return to FedEx, while the vision is about faster delivery, the mission is actually concerned with transforming the way people communicate. Second, vision needs to be bold and ambitious otherwise it will be viewed as an objective or organisational aim. If Fred Smith had articulated his vision as *Let's beat the US Post Office by 25 per cent*, it would not have had the same motivational impact on his staff and potential customers.

To create effective visioning through team working, organisations must develop a culture that is built on trust and is seen to reward creativity and diversity. Team members must develop a collective sense of responsibility and direction. Effective visioning requires a willingness to create all the options and to share information needed to develop them. It also demands that staff commit to a plan of action that is in the best interests of the organisation, even if this may result in unwelcome changes. Creating a visioning culture can be time-consuming because it can take up to five years to achieve, which may present problems when staff commitment and action is required over a shorter timescale. The link between visioning and leadership is simple: for vision to work, a champion is needed to inspire other participants and stakeholders. Clear, frequent and above all, personal communication is crucial if the vision is to be accepted and people to be inspired. Video messaging or email cannot distribute visions although they can be used to reinforce them. Finally, an experienced and credible team is necessary to shape, sell and drive the vision. In today's complex world, whether commercial business or health care, one person cannot know everything and do it all. Consequently, leadership teams are essential. They are also important if one person's views, with all their potential prejudices, are not to dominate the organisation or service.

Passion

Passion is also an important characteristic of leaders. It is an essential personal characteristic if potential followers are to be inspired. Although the popular view is that the voluntary and public sectors produce passionate leaders, increasingly the private sector and government are embracing it too. Indeed, passion is often an essential requirement for the successful political leader. Passion is important because people who are motivated and involved in pursuing a vision or task produce their best. And the best way to motivate others is to be both passionate and motivated yourself. Facts and quantitative analyses are important in generating support for change but so are emotions. Having said that, there is also a dark and dangerous side of passion. It can deceive, cloud judgement and destroy. History is littered with passionate political and organisational leaders who have pursued their personal aims to the detriment of their country or business. Passionate leadership requires the balancing of beliefs, risks and personal visions. Passion can create vitality and energy but it needs to be underpinned by trust, clear values and a preparedness to temper its dark side by assessing risk. Achieving that requires the leader to surround themselves with a strong and trusted team who are capable of counterbalancing the leader's views and opinions with their own. For chief executives and executives who operate corporately at board level, counterbalancing can be achieved by working with a team of experienced and independent non-executives with a focus on organisational governance.

LEADERS AND FOLLOWERS

Another essential element flowing from the definition of leadership is that the people involved in this relationship are leaders and followers. Since leaders can be anyone, so too can followers. That does not mean that leaders and followers are equal. A distinction between leaders and followers remains crucial to the concept of leadership. Since leadership is a relationship-based process, leaders must interact with other people; after all, leaders cannot exist without followers. If all the people with whom leaders interacted were other leaders, leadership as a meaningful construct would not make much sense. People who are active in the leadership process are followers. This is an important distinction from passive people who are not in a relationship because they have chosen not to be involved, they have no influence and therefore, they cannot be followers. In contrast, active people can fall anywhere on a continuum of activity from highly active to minimally active, and their influence in the leadership process is based on their level of activity, their willingness to get involved, and their use of the power resources they have at their disposal to influence other people.

There are also links between bad leaders and bad followers (Kellerman 2004). Bad leaders include those who act unethically because they cannot tell the difference between right and wrong. Leaders are also bad if they are incompetent, overly rigid, corrupt, callous, insular, evil and intemperate. According to Kellerman, bad leaders may display one or more of these characteristics. In contrast, good leaders are both effective and ethical in their approach. What is important to note is that if leaders are bad then so will be some of their followers, as history has shown only too well. In situations of actual or potential bad leadership, followers can strengthen their personal capacity to resist leaders who are ineffective or unethical by empowering themselves, being loyal to the whole and not to any single individual, being sceptical, taking a stand when necessary and paying attention. Above all else, followers should hold leaders to account.

Followers can become leaders and leaders can become followers in any one leadership relationship. People are not stuck in one or the other for the whole time the relationship exists. Followers may be leaders for a while, and leaders may be followers for a while. This is particularly so when groups are formed from across different organisations, where one organisation may take the lead for one part of an initiative and another organisation takes the lead for something else. This ability to change places without changing organisational positions gives followers considerable influence and mobility. In short, followers are not always followers in all leadership relationships. Finally, if we have leadership then is there such a thing as followership? One strongly held view is that followers do not do followership, they do leadership (Rost 1993). Both leaders and followers form one relationship, which is leadership; and consequentially, there is no such thing as followership. Followers and leaders develop a relationship in which they influence one another as well as their working environment, and that is leadership. They do not do the same things in the relationship, just as composers and musicians do not do the same thing in making music but they are both essential to success. But dissecting that is difficult, which is why leadership is one of the most observed yet least understood phenomena on earth.

GENDER AND LEADERSHIP

A frequently asked question is: are women and men different in how they think about leadership, how they practice it, and how others perceive them as leaders? Gender has been central to Western thought, entering virtually every domain of human experience and structuring human relationships. Gender categories are often used to organise our experiences since they allow us to define and categorise individuals. In *Women and Leadership*, Klenke (1996) reports little or no difference between men and women on the interpersonal versus task orientated leadership styles. However, comparisons of leader effectiveness favour men more and women less when three conditions are present (Northouse 2001): when the context is male dominated; when a high percentage of the leader's staff are male; and when the role is seen as more congenial to men in terms of self-assessed competence, interest and low requirements for cooperation coupled with high requirements for control. Effectiveness comparisons favour women leaders to the degree that these conditions are reversed. Further, effectiveness comparisons favour women leaders for second-level or middle management in business, education and government or social service, while they favour male leaders in first level or supervisory positions.

It is not surprising that the literature concludes, in the light of women tending to demonstrate less effective leadership skills in roles that are male-dominated, that women leaders are particularly devalued when they work in male-dominated environments and when their evaluators are men, even though women evaluators did not favour one sex over the other (Northouse ibid.). In their evaluation of the evidence of the female leadership advantage Eagly and Carli (2003) discuss the assertion that women are more likely than men to lead in a style that is effective under contemporary social conditions. Their evaluation of the evidence shows that women have some advantages in typical leadership style but suffer some disadvantages from prejudicial evaluations of their competence as leaders, especially in a masculine organisational context. Women used a more participative or democratic style and a less autocratic or directive style than men did, although this tendency declined in a highly male-dominated environment. Both men and women emphasised more the achievement of objectives when the number of leaders of their own sex dominated the environment. This should not be interpreted as the tendency of women to lead more democratically as either an advantage or disadvantage, since a democratic leadership style may enhance leader effectiveness under some circumstances, while the autocratic style may facilitate a leader's effectiveness under a different set of circumstances, for example during a crisis situation.

What the above means is that leadership styles divided along gender lines are less obvious. Concern for people may only become appropriate and acceptable to followers once attention to the vision and task has established the leader's credibility and defined a context for the interaction between the leader and followers. Finally, while overall effectiveness does not differ for leaders of either sex, female and male leaders may differ in the conditions that prove a good fit for their leadership style. Some men also experience discomfort with women leaders because they see them as perceiving a need to adapt their behavioural style so that men avoid feeling intimidated. Consequently, a narrower range of acceptable behaviour exists for female than for male leaders.

In the light of the above literature it is not surprising that prejudice about women leaders can have a direct impact on their careers. Female and male leaders differ in the lengths to which they must go to be promoted, in the need to adapt their behaviour at work, in the amount of support they tend to receive at work and the impact of family factors on career advancement. Women are more likely to be devalued when they comprise a small proportion of the numbers considered for promotion, when performance standards and information are ambiguous, when affirmative actions are perceived as influencing selection decisions and when organisational practices make demographic group membership pertinent. In other words, majority male cultures do not favour the advancement of women leaders. Personal barriers to female advancement refer to elements of their personal lives or a lack of knowledge that may be an obstacle. Women leaders have reported lower political personal skills as a factor that has impeded their advancement although other women executives have reported skills in building alliances and navigating the competing priorities affecting organisational decisions. Perhaps more serious for many women leaders are the home or non-work obligations for which in many societies they remain primarily responsible in a household. The need for better balance in the seeming impossibility of combining successful personal and professional lives has been a frequent theme in women leaders' descriptions of their lives. These tensions sometimes arise because of organisational conditions that put women at a disadvantage compared to their male peers (Northouse ibid.).

In addition to unsupportable corporate cultures that discourage balancing career aspirations with personal obligations, there are also cultures that dissuade women from applying for senior management or require women to accomplish major tasks without sufficient resources. It should not be surprising therefore that women can be viewed as less competent and disinterested in significant challenges with the consequence that unlike their male peers they need to actively seek challenging objectives rather than wait for them to be allocated. Nevertheless, more women are rising into leadership roles at all levels, including executive positions. They suggest that the reasons for this are multifactorial: in organisations, leadership roles have changed and practices that constituted barriers to promoting women into positions of authority have eroded; at a cultural level, appointments of female leaders have come to symbolise a progressive organisational culture; and women have changed by assuming the personal characteristics required to succeed in new organisational roles.

In examining women's leadership in developed and developing countries Klenke (ibid.) concluded that it makes little sense to group together as comparable the leadership of all countries of the Western world on the grounds that they are all democracies. The review highlights the importance of cultural specificity and context in shaping women's (and men's) leadership both domestically and internationally, which makes it difficult to generalise about female and male leaders. This may have implications for leadership development in Europe's less economically developed countries (culture is discussed further in Chapter 5 on emotional intelligence). What is more consistent with the contextual importance of leadership is not to ask the question, 'do female and male leaders act similarly?', but more importantly, 'in what context and under what conditions do female and male leaders act similarly?' The one certainty that does exist is that in the increasingly complex work environment of today and tomorrow, women and men need to learn the strength of each other's leadership styles and practices. They need to support each other's ways of leading as opposed to treating one approach as necessarily better than the other.

LINKS BETWEEN LEADERSHIP AND OTHER LITERATURE

Power

Power in organisations is open to many interpretations but essentially it is concerned with the ability or potential to influence (Fiol *et al.* 2001). Although the literature on power discusses consequences for individuals and groups, it does not provide a model tracing the linkages between them and how power develops and is transferred between them. The power literature introduces 'power mental models', which are organised mental representations in the minds of individuals about their power and that of others. These tend to lead to relatively predictable behaviours within a particular context. Power mental models (PMMs) can be subdivided into models about individuals and their groups, called 'identity PMMs' and 'reputation PMMs'. The former is a unit's own set of beliefs about how powerful it is, while a reputation PMM is the set of beliefs about how powerful the unit is. Importantly, these models do not develop in isolation and individuals develop power bases through social interaction.

Fiol *et al.* (ibid.) propose a cross-level and multi-level approach, the value of which lies in the explicit recognition that individual- and group-level power are not independent of each other but are mutually affected in critical ways.

This means that failure to recognise that these inter-relationships may result in practical interventions at one level producing a negative or neutral result because of the unanticipated influences of other levels. Further, there are strong linkages between power identity and power reputation. The transfer of power across organisational levels can occur when a less powerful group gains power because of the presence of a powerful new member; the same can potentially happen when a less powerful person gains power because of their membership in a powerful group. There are links here with leadership and the management of change involving the formation of new groups or the realignment of power and decision-making across an inter-organisational or network-based system. The most important consequence of linking the power and leadership litera-tures is the need for future research to focus on power not only within but also between organisational levels as well as between organisations.

Trust

The trust literature shows, among other things, the difficulties of working across organisational boundaries and securing support for change from stakeholders over whom there is no hierarchical or managerial control. Consequently the development of trust and cooperation can be difficult because of conflicting objectives. This raises the question of whether group membership is an affec-tive or emotional context for trust development (Williams 2001). Motivation to trust is defined as the desire to view another person as trustworthy enough to be relied upon. In turn, people who view others as trustworthy enough see this as one way of attempting to build and maintain social relations. In general, we develop the trustworthiness of others by interacting with them over time and specifically from our perceptions of their ability, benevolence, integrity and honesty. It is not surprising therefore that people use their feelings as informa-tion when making judgements about others. There are links here with emotional intelligence, which is discussed in Chapter 5.

Williams argues that traditional managerial approaches to developing trust, and thereby improving cooperation and coordination are increasingly inappro-priate to rapidly changing environments. These approaches include reward systems and structuring tasks in ways that promote individual identification with an inclusive group such as the project or organisation. In contrast, what is required is the need to attend to the affective context of work interactions; for example, managers who articulate sources of negative feeling such as stress related to a change programme may be able to decrease its impact by referring to the difficulty of the change programme rather than the behaviour or person-ality of others. Consequently, this could decrease negative influences on the evaluation of the trustworthiness of other people when change involves people from different departments, services or organisations. Therefore, the expression of negative feelings and the reasons for those feelings may represent an effective but underused leadership skill at times of change. Trust is discussed in more detail in Chapter 4 on networks, partnership and collaboration.

THE MYTHS OF LEADERSHIP

In the light of the long and complex history of leadership it is not surprising that myths about leaders and leadership have emerged (Goffee and Jones 2000). The most well-known and persistent myth is that leadership is associated with superior position and therefore restricted to small numbers of people. It is a myth that when you are in charge of your organisation or service you are automatically a leader. The people who make it to senior positions may have done so because of self-promotion rather than because of personal leadership qualities and delivery of positive change. They may have networked their way to the top or just been in the right place at the right time when promotion opportunities arose. Remember that luck plays its part in most careers to some extent. This chapter has emphasised that leadership is not about position – it is about process, relationships and influence. Leadership involves personal skills and abilities that are useful irrespective of organisational or hierarchical position.

The next myth is that not everyone can be a leader, but this is only because many executives and managers do not have the self-knowledge or the authenticity for leadership. Developing self-knowledge is discussed further in Chapter 5. Another popular myth is that leaders will deliver the required results. This is not always the case because some well-led organisations do not necessarily produce short-term results while conversely, some organisations with successful results are not necessarily well led. If results were always a matter of good leadership, choosing leaders would be easy for both the public and private sectors. Finally, there is the myth that leaders are good coaches. This is not always true but it has not prevented the idea growing that good leadership equals good coaching. This somewhat simplistic belief rests on the assumption that a single person can both inspire people and impart the necessary technical and leadership skills. Today's world is complex with its increasing dependency on inter-organisational collaboration for the achievement of results and the management of relationships. Consequently, personal and organisational success is dependent upon the development of individual leadership skills coupled with the creation of sustainable and high-calibre leadership teams to both support and complement the skills of the individual leader. One person can no longer do it all.

CONCLUSION

Understanding leadership can be difficult, which partly explains why academics argue that leadership has proved to be one of the most appealing yet more challenging subjects within management research. This is largely because of two difficulties. First, as is clearly seen from the literature, leadership is not solely about command and control and the obedience of followers. Second, leadership cannot be understood in any significant way when it is reduced to the sweeping generalisations of the biography of the business or political leader. It is much more complex than that. Although the exploration of leadership tells us that it is resistant to unambiguous definition, what can be stated with certainty is that leadership is about three components: the leader, the followers and the context within which the leader and followers work. Context is very important because it raises the question, not whether leaders make a difference but under what conditions they can make a difference. However, as yet there has been little work on the impact of organisational leadership under different conditions.

Leadership has more to do with personal authenticity than an easily learned approach to be used at all times and in all situations. The real personal challenge for aspiring leaders is to be true to themselves and not merely to copy the habits of some other leader. It is important to remember that ongoing personal learning is an essential part of the leadership process for everyone involved, whether new or experienced leader, follower or stakeholder. Experienced leaders know that no two work situations are the same and people's behaviour in any given situation can never be wholly predicted. Learning from each situation is therefore important for future personal leadership development. Unfortunately, the persistent and popular view of leadership has too many connotations of individualism and heroism. We have to surrender the myth of leadership as an isolated, heroic activity and replace it with leadership distributed among other individuals and teams within and between organisations.

The job of leaders at the top of organisations is to create the culture and systems under which others are encouraged and motivated to lead themselves. Organisations that will be the most successful in the future will be those in which it is everyone's job to be creating and using ideas for positive change. Most managers will not know all the answers but they will not have to do all the work of leadership by themselves. Shared leadership means empowering individuals at all levels and giving them the opportunity to take the lead. This is now becoming more common as top-down organisational structures give way to flatter, more decentralised and network-based forms, which is seen as a way of promoting intra- and inter-organisational collaboration and partnership.

Although shared leadership can happen anywhere within an organisation or between organisations it tends to develop where there is a number of partnerships and alliances both within and between organisations where managers work jointly on specific projects or assignments. Flatter organisational structures mean the sharing of responsibility and accountability throughout – and increasingly between – organisations working collaboratively so that power, authority and decision-making are more dispersed, both laterally and vertically. Given that inter-organisational working is more important than ever before for personal and organisational leadership success it is unfortunate that inter-organisational aspects of leadership and consequently, inter-organisational influence, have largely been ignored in most studies and definitions of leadership. In today's more complex, networked and systems-based world a more appropriate definition of leadership would be as follows:

> Leadership is a dynamic process of pursuing a vision for change in which the leader is supported by two main groups: followers within the leader's own organisation, and influential players and other organisations operating in the leader's wider, external environment.
>
> (Goodwin 2002)

Today's generation of female and male leaders, compared to those of previous generations are more likely to be open to consensus building, participative decision-making, and delegation of responsibility and the empowerment of followers. The preoccupation of the last century with leadership tasks is now being replaced by an emphasis on people issues such as the mutuality and reciprocity of leader–follower relations. Today's leaders are likely to create and communicate a shared vision of the future that not only creates a common ground among people of differing views but also responds creatively to an environment of ongoing societal and organisational change. At a macro-political level this is reflected in the societal changes of the former communist countries of Europe. However, although the broader socio-political context of leadership may be different from what it was 50 years ago, leadership skills are still an essential prerequisite to its practice and the achievement of results. We should not lose sight of leadership being a means to an organisational end and not an end in itself: leadership remains concerned with the achievement of results. But if one leadership skill is to be emphasised above others then it is influence. This is because much of the leader's activity, irrespective of the context, involves attempts to influence the attitudes and behaviour of others. In essence, leadership as an influence-based relationship activity that has two characteristics:

- first, it is multi-directional in that influence flows in all directions and not just up and down the hierarchy;
- second, it is non-coercive, meaning that it is based not on managerial or positional authority or power but on personal persuasive behaviours and actions, which allows anyone in the leader–follower relationship to freely agree or disagree and ultimately to drop into or out of the relationship.

The complexity and understanding of leadership is pursued further in Chapter 2, which discusses leadership models and styles.

DISCUSSION QUESTIONS

1 Do you understand the difference between management and leadership? Can you identify examples of both in your organisation and do you know when each is happening and why? What can you personally learn from your observations?
2 Do you know when you are operating in managerial and leadership roles? Are you aware of the additional personal skills you bring into use when operating as a leader?
3 Do you have a vision for the future of your organisation or service? Is it exciting and motivational and can you articulate it clearly to others around you?
4 Do you see examples of leadership teams in action – perhaps you lead or participate in one? Can you observe how the leader and the team members interact and work together?
5 Do you see the differences that leaders and their teams have on the work of your organisation, network or service?
6 Do you have the opportunity to observe female and male leaders in action and do you see any differences between the two?
7 Can you see examples of powerful people in leadership positions in networks and understand why they are powerful?
8 What do you understand by trust in your professional work? Do you think your work colleagues would have the same understanding?

BIBLIOGRAPHY AND FURTHER READING

Alimo-Metcalfe B. and Lawler J. (2001) Leadership development in UK companies at the beginning of the twenty-first century. Lessons for the NHS? *Journal of Management in Medicine* 15(5): 387–404.

Antrobus S. and Kitson A. (1999) Nursing leadership: influencing and shaping health policy and nursing practice. *Journal of Advanced Nursing* 29(3): 746–753.

Bass B.M. (1990) *Bass and Stogdill's Handbook of Leadership Theory, Research and Managerial Applications*. New York: The Free Press.

Bennis W.G. and Thomas R.J. (2002) *Geeks and Geezers*. Boston: Harvard Business School Press.

Bresnen M.J. (1995) All things to all people? Perceptions, attributions, and constructions of leadership. *Leadership Quarterly* 6(4): 495–513.

Checkland P. (1985) From optimizing to learning: a development of systems thinking for the 1990s. *Journal of Operational Research Society* 36(9): 757–767.

Dawson S. (1996) *Analysing Organisations*. Basingstoke: Palgrave.

Eagly H. and Carli L.L. (2003) The female leadership advantage: an evaluation of the evidence. *The Leadership Quarterly* 14: 807–834.

Fiol C.M., O'Connor E.J. and Aguinis H. (2001) All for one and one for all? The development and transfer of power across organisational levels. *Academy of Management Review* 26(2): 224–242.

Goffee R. and Jones G. (2000) Why should anyone be led by you? *Harvard Business Review* September–October: 62–70.

Goodwin N. (2002) *The Leadership Role of Chief Executives in the English NHS*. University of Manchester: PhD thesis.

Kakabadse A. and Kakabadse N. (1999) *Essence of Leadership*. London: International Thomson Business Press.

Kellerman B. (2004) *Bad Leadership: what it is, how it happens, why it matters*. Boston: Harvard Business School Press.

Klenke K. (1996) *Women and Leadership. A contextual perspective*. New York: Springer Publishing Company.

Kotter J.P. (1990) What leaders really do. *Harvard Business Review* May–June: 103–111.

Lieberson S. and O'Connor J. (1972) Leadership and organisational performance: a study of large corporations. *American Sociological Review* 37: 117–130.

Mintzberg H. (1989) *Mintzberg on Management, Inside Our Strange World of Organisations*. New York: The Free Press.

Northouse P.G. (2001) *Leadership Theory and Practice*, 2nd edn. London: Sage.

Pettigrew A., Ferlie E. and McKee L. (1994) *Shaping Strategic Change, Making Change in Large Organisations: the case of the National Health Service*. London: Sage.

Pfeffer J. (1982) *Organisations and Organisation Theory*. Boston, MA: Pitman.

Pfeffer J. (1997) The Ambiguity of Leadership. *Academy of Management Review* January 1997: 104–112.

Rost J.C. (1993) *Leadership for the Twenty-First Century*. London: Praeger.

Thomas A.B. (1988) Does leadership make a difference to organisational perform-ance? *Administrative Science Quarterly* 33: 388–400.

Wheatley M.J. (1999) *Leadership and the New Science. Discovering order in a chaotic world*. San Francisco: Berrett-Koehler Publishers.

Williams M. (2001) In whom we trust: group membership as an affective context for trust development. *Academy of Management Review* 26(3): 377–396.

Yukl G. (1994) *Leadership in Orgnisations*. New Jersey: Prentice-Hall.

Chapter 2

Leadership movements and models

KEY POINTS OF THIS CHAPTER

- There are numerous leadership theories but they are not conclusive about the nature of leadership.
- Until the advent of contingency theory in the 1960s, initial theories of leadership focused on whether there was a single, best type of leadership.
- Leadership is not radically different in the private and public sectors but historically there have been differences of emphasis.
- Leadership research needs to develop as a strong inter-disciplinary area of study in its own right rather than as a sub-set of other disciplines.
- There are many myths about leadership, which add to its complexity and our lack of understanding of its true nature.
- Most research has focused within organisations and consequently, we know less about inter-organisational leadership, which is now an important feature of the operating context of the health care sector.
- Academia has failed to develop a school of leadership that clearly articulates an understanding of what leadership actually is.

KEY TERMS

- ■ Trait and style theories
- ■ Situation or context
- ■ Contingency and path–goal theories
- ■ Charismatic leadership
- ■ Bad leadership
- ■ Transformational leadership

INTRODUCTION

This chapter builds on the overview of the first chapter by summarising the history of leadership studies to date including the numerous movements and models. Repeated studies do not show whether leaders fill their positions because they have inbuilt characteristics such as intelligence, originality, social participation and status, or whether the characteristics are nurtured by their personal experience of leadership. This takes us back to the 'born or made' argument with almost endless debate about whether leaders are born with characteristics such as energy and intelligence; or alternatively, if appropriate leadership behaviour can be learned. The answer to the born or made debate is that it is highly likely to be both and consequently, the debate is unnecessary because most individuals who either occupy or aspire to occupy leadership roles do benefit from encouragement and personal development. When we think of leadership we tend most often to think of personality. Historically, the focus on personality in leadership studies has been American dominated. In contrast, Europeans have tried to resist such personification of leadership and consequently, they have conceded the majority of the field of leadership studies to the USA, which owned the subject for most of the second half of the last century.

THE THEORIES OF LEADERSHIP

Trait theories

At the beginning of the last century most countries, with few exceptions, were governed by the ruling classes, which gave rise to the Great Man theory of leadership. The theory was based on the belief that these men (and almost without exception they were men) were born into the leadership role and therefore possessed the required personal qualities to become leaders. In addition, it was believed that these traits could only be inherited and not learnt. It was following the Great Man theory that trait theory emerged in the 1920s. It represented the first serious leadership research and focused on attempts to identify the traits, qualities and attributes of effective leaders.

Researchers observed leaders to try and determine what gave them their inborn superiority. Research continued up until the 1940s when it became accepted that although prominent leaders may be gifted, they did not possess a universal set of leadership characteristics. This was because it was eventually realised that the personal qualities and attributes of those in leadership positions were also shared by a wider, diverse group of people who were not in leadership positions. Consequently, trait theory lost most of its momentum by the time of the Second World War.

The style theory

This was the next theory to emerge, arguing that one particular style of leadership was the most effective. The theory reflected the spirit of post-Second World War America with its emphasis on openness, democracy and meritocracy. The style approach to leadership concentrates on overtly observable leader behaviour rather than inferred psychological traits and in that respect it is different from the trait approach. Style researchers determined that leadership was composed of essentially two kinds of behaviour: task behaviours and relationship behaviours. The former facilitates the achievement of objectives while relationship behaviours help followers feel comfortable with themselves, with each other and with their work situation. Therefore, the underlying approach of the style theory is to explain how leaders combine these two kinds of behaviour to influence people in their efforts to meet objectives.

There are three principal sources of research into leadership traits, which are comprehensively summarised by Northouse (2001): first, the work at Ohio State University, which is based on the findings of Ralph Stogdill in the 1940s; second, the University of Michigan, which explored how leadership functioned in small groups; and the third and probably most well known to practising managers, the work of Blake and Mouton in the 1960s, who explored how managers used task and relationship behaviours in their work. The Ohio State studies analysed how individuals acted when they were leading a group or organisation using questionnaires completed by staff. It was found that staff views focused on two general types of leader behaviour: initiating structure and consideration. As the term implies, the former were essentially task behaviours such as providing structure to the context of the work, organising and scheduling the work and defining responsibilities. In contrast, consideration behaviours were essentially relationship behaviours and included building respect, liking between the leader and followers, trust and group camaraderie. In summary, the research concluded that leaders provide first, structure for their staff and second, they nurture them. Importantly, these two behaviours were believed to be both distinct and independent and not connected. This meant that a leader could be high in initiating structure and high or low in task behaviour or vice versa. Studies undertaken since then have tried to determine which style of leadership is most effective in a particular situation or context. Not surprisingly, in some situations high consideration has been found to be most effective but in other situations high initiating structure has been found to be effective.

Research undertaken at the same time by the University of Michigan identified two types of leader behaviours called 'employee orientation' and 'production orientation'. As the term implies, employee orientation describes the behaviour of leaders with a strong human relations emphasis such as taking an interest in staff personally and valuing their individuality and personal needs, which is very similar to the Ohio State consideration behaviour. In contrast, production orientation refers to leadership behaviour that stresses the technical and production aspects of a job, meaning staff are viewed as a means for achieving work objectives; again similar to Ohio State's initiating structure. The most important difference between the Michigan and Ohio State research is that the former initially concluded that employee and production orientation are opposite ends of a single continuum suggesting that leaders who were production orientated were less concerned about employees and vice versa. However, as more studies were completed Michigan concluded that their two constructs were similar to the Ohio State studies and independent of each other.

Blake and Mouton's managerial or leadership grid is probably the most well-known model of managerial behaviour. It first appeared in the early 1960s and is a good example of a practical model of leadership. It conceptualised leadership in the form of a managerial grid with two axes: one for task and the other for people (Bass 1990). As the term implies, concern for production reflects a leader's concern with achieving organisational objectives such as developing new products, processing work and developing policy. Concern for people refers to a leader's attention to people who are trying to achieve objectives. The concerns include building commitment and trust, providing good working conditions and fair pay, and promoting good social relations. By plotting concerns for production and concerns for people on the two intersecting axes people may be high or low on both axes or they may be high on one and low on the other. The leader who rates high on both axes develops followers who are committed to the accomplishment of work and have a sense of interdependence through a common stake in the organisation's objectives. Equally important, relationships of respect and trust for the leader also emerge.

The overall conclusion from Blake and Mouton's work is that a person in the work situation usually has a dominant style, in other words one that he or she will use in most situations. Leaders will also have a back-up style, which is reverted to when the leader is under pressure; most often when the usual way of getting things done does not work. The style approach was a major step forward in leadership research, moving it on from leadership being seen almost exclusively as a personality trait to a framework for assessing leadership in a broader way. It does not work by telling leaders how to behave but by describing the major components of their behaviour. Leaders are reminded that their actions toward others occur on both task and relationship levels. In some situations, leaders need to be more task orientated, while in others they need to be more relationship orientated. Above all else, the style approach expanded leadership research to include what leaders did and how they acted. However, its main weakness, in common with a lot of leadership research, is that it is not able to link leadership style, organisational performance and variables such as staff morale, job satisfaction, productivity and efficiency (Yukl 1994).

The situational approach

A further criticism of the style approach is that it has been unable to identify the universal behaviours that are associated with effective leadership. This is similar to the trait approach, which was unable to identify the definitive personal characteristics of leaders. These criticisms emerged because it has been impossible to find a universal style of leadership that could be implemented in almost every situation, which led to the new theory of situational leadership emerging. As the term implies, situational leadership focuses on leadership in situations; it is based on the work of John Hersey and Kenneth Blanchard (Bass 1990). The theory is that different situations demand different kinds of leadership and for the leader to be effective requires adapting his or her style to the demands of different situations. Situational leadership emphasises that leadership is composed of both a directive and a supportive dimension and each has to be applied appropriately in a given situation. This involves a leader assessing how competent and committed staff are to performing a given task.

On the assumption that the skills and motivation of staff vary over time, situational leadership suggests that leaders should change the degree to which they are directive or supportive to meet the changing needs of their subordinates

(Northouse ibid.). In other words, situational leadership requires the leader to match his or her style to the competence, commitment and maturity of their staff. Effective leaders are seen as those who can recognise what staff need and then adapt their own style to meet those needs. As staff mature and become more competent and experienced in their work then the leader's behaviour should be characterised by a decreasing emphasis on consideration. This means that situational leadership requires leaders to treat each person differently based on the task to be undertaken and to seek opportunities to help them learn new skills and become more confident in their work. Overall, situational leadership emphasises that staff have unique needs and should be helped in trying to become better at doing their work. Situational leadership does have its weaknesses, mainly because there have only been a few research studies conducted to justify its assumptions and propositions (Bass ibid.; Northouse ibid.).

Contingency theory

In some ways a development of situational leadership, contingency theory is aimed at matching leaders to appropriate situations. The work of Fred Fiedler is the most cited and his work dominated much of the leadership research in the 1970s (Bass ibid.; Dawson 1996; Northouse ibid.). It is called contingency theory because it suggests that the leader's effectiveness depends on how well their style fits the context. It is therefore a contextual theory of leadership. Within contingency theory, leadership styles are described as task motivated or relationship motivated. Further, situations are characterised by the assessment of three factors: the leader–member relations, the task structure and position power. Leader–member relations refers to the group atmosphere and the degree of confidence, loyalty and attraction that followers feel for their leader; and it was Fiedler's view that the relationship between the leader and the group was the most important variable. Task structure refers to the degree to which the requirements of a task are clearly defined and understood by those required to perform them in terms of process and outcome. Position power refers to the amount of authority a leader has to reward or to punish staff, including the legitimate power the leader has as a result of their position in an organisation or hierarchy. Position power is strong if the leader has authority to hire and fire, promote people or alter their pay; conversely, it is weak if the leader does not have the right to do these things. Fiedler argues that at the extremes of high or low situational control, the task-orientated leader is the most effective; while in between the extremes a people-orientated leader works best.

Although true that leadership style is dependent upon a particular situation the problem is that there are many situations in life and work that influence the way we behave. Consequently, contingency theory fails to explain fully why individuals with certain leadership styles are more effective in some situations than in others; and also fails to explain what organisations should do when there is a mismatch between the leader and the situation. One of the main problems with contingency theory is that it does not advocate teaching leaders how to adapt their styles to various situations so that leadership and the achievement of organisational objectives can be improved. Rather, the theory advocates that leaders engage in situational engineering, in essence changing situations to fit the leader. However, most practising managers would say that this is naive, particularly in organisations or services such as health care that are heavily context driven by factors such as government policy and consumer demand. What is perhaps more achievable is to explore adapting a situation, such as an imposed government policy, to 'fit' the local context.

In the light of the above comments, it is not surprising that although contingency theory is supported by a great deal of empirical research (Northouse ibid.). Fiedler's research has been criticised for only examining a limited range of unusual groups such as basketball teams and bomber crews; and organisational life tends to be more complicated than a game of basketball. However, the most important contribution of contingency theory has been to broaden the understanding of leadership by forcing us to consider the impact of situations on leaders. Before contingency theory was developed, leadership theories focused on whether there was a single, best type of leadership. In contrast, contingency theory emphasises the importance of focusing on the relationship between the leader's style and the demands of various situations. Consequently, by its focus on the link between the leader and situations, contingency theory shifted the emphasis of leadership research from person–person to person–context.

Path–goal theory

This theory focuses on how leaders motivate their staff to accomplish designated goals. The theory, which draws heavily on motivation theory, appeared in the 1970s (Dawson ibid.; Northouse ibid.) and is aimed at enhancing staff performance and satisfaction by focusing on staff motivation. The theory argues that leaders are effective if they can help followers identify an objective and then enable them to achieve it. While the situational approach suggests a leader must adapt to the development level of subordinates and contingency theory emphasises a match between a leader's style and specific situational variables, path–goal theory emphasises the relationship between a leader's style and the characteristics of staff and the work setting. The underlying assumption of path–goal theory is derived from expectancy theory, which suggests that staff will be motivated if they think they are capable of performing their work; if they believe their efforts will result in a certain outcome; and if they believe the pay-offs for doing their work are worthwhile. For the leader, the challenge is to use a leadership style that best meets the motivational needs of staff by choosing behaviours that complement or supplement what is missing in the work setting. So, leaders try to enhance the achievement of staff objectives by providing information or rewards. It is argued that leadership generates motivation when it increases the number and kinds of rewards that staff receive from their work. Leadership also motivates when it makes the path to achieving the objective clear and easy to travel through coaching and direction; when it removes obstacles to achieving the objective; and when it makes the work itself more personally satisfying.

Above all, path–goal theory provides a model that is very practical because it emphasises the need for leaders to clarify and help staff achieve organisational objectives, which is a key leadership responsibility. A significant criticism however of path–goal theory is that it fails to explain adequately the relationship between leadership behaviour and staff motivation. The theory is unique because it incorporates expectancy theory but it does not go far enough in explaining how leadership is related to that theory. The principles of expectancy theory suggest that staff will be motivated if they feel competent and trust that their efforts will get results, but path–goal theory does not describe how a leader could employ various styles directly to assist staff to feel competent or assured of success. Further, path–goal theory is very staff orientated in that it underscores the importance of leaders providing coaching, guidance and overall direction as well as helping staff to define and clarify goals and to help them around obstacles. In effect, the theory treats leadership as a one-way event and therefore the potential difficulty of the theory is that it over-promotes the dependency of staff without recognising the scope to achieve their full potential through personal self-development (Northouse ibid.).

It can be seen already from this chapter that one of the obvious problems with leadership theories is that they are presented as separate and distinct movements. The reality is that there is much overlap between theories; the movements and associated models are not distinct from one another and the suggestion that each has a beginning and an end is incorrect (Rost 1993). What the above theories do show is that leadership is concerned with tasks, relationships and situations (which is also referred to as context or environment). However, in addition to context and tasks, we also see that leadership and leaders cannot exist without followers; and to create potential followers requires a vision to inspire them with a view of the future that they find exciting and empathetic. In turn, vision and inspiration inevitably generate thoughts about charismatic leadership. These issues are now briefly explored before considering the final and most recent theory, which is transformational leadership.

Charismatic leadership

Theories about charismatic leadership have been around for over 50 years and there is an overlap with transformational leadership, which is also discussed below (Conger and Kanungo 1998). Charisma is a personal trait attributed to the leader by followers, and in that regard it is no different from the attribution of leadership generally made to an individual exercising the maximum influence over a group. Personal characteristics of a charismatic leader include being dominant, having a strong desire to influence others, being self-confident and having a strong sense of their own moral values. In addition, charismatic leaders tend to be strong role-models for the beliefs and values they want their followers to adopt. Examples of well-known charismatic leaders include Ghandi, Martin Luther King Jr, John F. Kennedy, Winston Churchill and Adolf Hitler. What charismatic leadership generates is: trust in a leader's ideology; warmth towards the leader; follower obedience; identification with the leader including emotional involvement in the leader's aims; and, for followers, heightened aims and confidence in the achievement of aims. In short, charismatic leaders seek to demonstrate that they have a total dedication to the course they share with their followers. The leader's actions are frequently seen by followers to involve greater personal risk, cost and energy and consequently, charismatic leaders create strong perceptions that they are highly trustworthy, which in turn solidifies follower commitments to them and their mission.

Charismatic leadership does have a dark side and one of the greatest risks is the charismatic leader extending themselves further and further until failure results. This is because of the situation the charismatic leader finds themselves in or because of the leader's personal weaknesses (Bass 1990: 201; Conger and Kanungo ibid.). For example, the high profile failings of companies like Enron are often because of a mix of charisma and greed, coupled with the misuse of the centralisation of power and leaders losing touch with reality by beginning to believe their own publicity. Leaders develop considerably heightened self-belief and self-importance, becoming complacent and grandiose, denying reality and losing their personal sense of morality. The risks increase the longer the leader remains in a position of power. Failure is often brought about by a lack of proportion, the absence of any real and sustained grip on reality and extreme narcissism, which is exacerbated by surrounding themselves with sycophantic, non-questioning followers. The strength of the charismatic leader's personality may discourage people from telling the truth and they will often ignore it when it is expressed. Similarly, charisma can blind people to the failings of an individual or their arguments. Another risk for the charismatic leader, who will derive their energy from the change they propose to pursue, is taking little interest in the need for effective administration or management and in developing the leadership ability of people around them. Consequently, they may invest little of their time and attention in designing effective control systems, establishing performance management or structuring roles and responsibilities, because these activities appear to hold little personal interest (Conger and Kanungo ibid.). Charismatic leaders may also be unwilling to develop others to be equal to themselves in terms of personal leadership capability and power. It is therefore not surprising that there are potentially considerable succession challenges associated with charismatic leadership. These challenges flow from the culture of dependence generated by the charismatic leader that impedes the opportunity for followers to develop similar leadership capabilities.

The book *Bad Leadership* (Kellerman 2004) suggests a number of ways leaders can strengthen their personal capability and capacity to be more effective and ethical in their leadership. However, to be successful requires self-awareness and so there are links with emotional intelligence (see Chapter 5). If possible, leaders in powerful positions should have limited tenure, perhaps similar to politicians and some presidents in democratic countries. Delegation and collaboration with others is important in minimising the risks of bad leadership. Team members need to be appointed who complement the leader's own knowledge, strengths and weaknesses. Further, leaders should encourage openness in which a diversity of views and dissent are encouraged; to do so however requires considerable personal maturity because not everybody responds well to personal challenge.

The chief problem with charismatic leadership is that we have fallen in love with the idea of the celebrity chief executive, those charismatic individuals who swoop in to save organisations and then appear frequently in the media because they are much more interesting to read and write about. Given this popular interest do charismatic leaders have a more significant effect on the overall performance of the organisation they lead? Waldman *et al.* (2001) hypothesised, in their study of 48 'Fortune 500' firms, that both transactional leadership and charisma are important aspects of strategic leadership, specifically that charisma adds to the effect of transactional leadership on organisational performance. In fact, after controlling for issues such as organisational size and chief executive tenure they found that neither transactional leadership nor charisma accounted for significant variation in organisational performance. However, a difference was seen when the researchers introduced the moderating effect of environmental uncertainty into the analysis, which is an individual's inability to understand the direction in which an environment is changing. The reason for introducing this variable flowed from the premise that a potentially charismatic relationship between chief executive and followers may allay follower concerns and generate confidence, especially as other studies had raised the possibility that environmental uncertainty may foster the emergence of charismatic leadership. The research results indicate that charismatic leadership interacting with organisational uncertainty is a key variable in the prediction of performance, findings that are consistent with previous research.

The antithesis of the modern charismatic leader is the one whose principle personal characteristic is humility. One example of the humble leader is Darwin E. Smith, who is discussed in the book, *Good to Great* (Collins 2001). In 1971 this ordinary man became chief executive of the paper company, Kimberly Clark, which for 100 years had never been wholly successful. The organisation had mediocre performance with returns to investors falling to 36 per cent behind the general stock market over the 20 years before Smith became chief executive. Over the next 20 years Smith led a stunning turnaround, generating returns to investors that beat the stock market by over four times. However, despite being one of the greatest chief executives of the last century, Darwin Smith remains largely unknown. Shy, reserved and self-effacing, Smith shunned any attempt to shine the spotlight on him, preferring instead to direct attention to Kimberly Clark and its people.

Darwin Smith was not weak and he took big decisions. He decided to sell all the traditional paper mills, which was the basis for the majority of Kimberly Clark's business, and invested all the money into the consumer paper business. It was a huge and painful step and he was derided for the decision. But his determination was the key to success and Kimberly Clark became the number one paper-based consumer products company in the world. Every good-to-great organisation in Collins' study has a similar leader to Darwin Smith. They are all self-effacing individuals who deflected adulation yet who had an almost stoic resolve to do whatever it took to make their organisations great. In summary, this was a paradoxical blend of personal humility and strong professional will. They were ambitious but their ambition was first and foremost for the organisation and its greatness, not for themselves. According to Collins, Darwin Smith never viewed himself as a hero and was a man who never entirely erased his own self-doubts, summing up his tenure at Kimberly Clark with what was said to be characteristic insight, 'I never stopped trying to become qualified for the job'.

Transformational leadership

This is the most contemporary leadership theory, which has been the focus of considerable research since the 1980s. Transformational leadership is a process that changes and transforms individuals; it is concerned with values, ethics, and standards. Importantly, the process also focuses on longer- rather than shorter-term goals (Burns 1979). Transformational leadership involves treating followers as full human beings with their own needs and motivation. The process seeks to win hearts and minds, to offer a vision, a sense of purpose and direction; as such, transformational leadership subsumes charismatic and visionary leadership. Most importantly, although transformational leadership plays a pivotal role in precipitating change, followers and leaders are inexorably bound together in the transformation process. For transformational leaders to be effective they must project their ideas onto images that excite people, resulting in choices being developed that turn the ideas into substance: in other words, the vision. The leader's role is to create an environment in which people can grow and contribute all their talents to the performance of the organisation or service.

Transformational leadership contrasts with other leadership models, which are essentially transactional in nature, meaning they appeal to individual self-interest by focusing on exchanges for mutual benefit between leaders and their followers. Transactional leadership involves managing in the conventional sense of clarifying the responsibilities of individuals, rewarding them for meeting objectives and correcting them for failing to meet objectives; for example, leaders who promise rewards to staff for achieving or exceeding their objectives are pursuing transactional leadership – 'you do something for me and I will do something for you'. In contrast, transformational leadership is a process in which the leader engages with potential followers as individual people. The connection ultimately becomes moral in that it raises the level of human conduct and ethical aspiration of both leader and followers and thus it has a transforming effect on both. The leader is attentive to the needs and motives of followers and tries to help them reach their fullest potential. An example of transformational leadership in the work setting would be a manager who attempts to change his or her organisational values to reflect a more human standard of fairness and justice. In the process, both the manager and followers may emerge with a stronger and higher set of moral values (Northouse ibid.). Well-known examples would include Martin Luther King Jr whose 'I Have a Dream' speech was a highly charismatic act, and the Indian leader Ghandi, who aroused and elevated the hopes and demands of millions of Indians, and whose own life and personality were enhanced in the process.

Vision is a focal point for transformational leadership. It provides the leader and followers with a map for where the organisation is going; it provides meaning and clarifies the identity of the organisation. Equally as important, vision provides followers with a sense of identity and a sense of self-efficacy. Transformational leadership, with its close association to charisma, has considerable appeal as the many biographies of charismatic political, business and sports leaders testify. For many people, transformational leadership makes sense partly because of its focus on a vision for the future. Transformational leadership also complements transactional-based leadership models with their emphasis on the exchange of rewards with the leader's attention to the needs and development of followers. However, transformational leadership has several weaknesses. The main criticism is that it lacks conceptual clarity because it covers such a wide range including creating a vision, motivating, being a change agent, building trust, and providing personal support and nurturance (Northouse ibid.). There is also the possibility that transformational leadership can be seen as a personality trait rather than a behaviour in which people can be instructed. If it is viewed as a trait, training people in transformational leadership is problematic because it is difficult to teach people how to change their personal characteristics; although developing emotional intelligence will help (see Chapter 5).

Another criticism is that transformational leadership may be seen to be elitist and anti-democratic because transformational leaders often play a direct role in creating change, establishing a vision and advocating new directions. This gives the impression that the leader is acting independently of followers or putting themselves above the needs of followers. History is littered with examples of political and business leaders who appear to have acted in this way and consequently, failed. Bass (1985) has provided a more expanded and refined version of transformational leadership by giving more attention to followers' rather than leaders' needs. He has suggested that transformational leadership could apply to situations in which the outcomes were not positive, and by describing transactional and transformational leadership as a single continuum rather than being independent as Burns (ibid.) did. Consequently, a leader could be both transformational and transactional and finally, as Conger and Kanungo (1998: 14) point out, Bass argues that charisma is a necessary ingredient of transformational leadership but by itself it is not sufficient to account for the transformational process.

LEADERSHIP IN THE PUBLIC SECTOR

Leadership is not radically different in the private and public sectors but historically there have been differences of emphasis, which to a certain extent continue to be seen even if the managerial cultures of the two sectors appear to be converging. The differences of emphasis have historically been seen as innovation and entrepreneurship, motivation, stability and power (Lane 2000); but the reality is that within the public sector health care provision and its management have been changing significantly during the last two decades and will continue to change even more with a blurring of the boundaries between the public and private sectors (discussed further in Chapter 3).

Innovation and entrepreneurship

It is often argued that public sector leaders are slow to innovate and adopt an entrepreneurial style because they are preoccupied with maintaining the status quo by following established systems, procedures and bureaucracy. However, this is changing. Five UK case studies highlight the development of civic entrepreneurship in the public sector, arguing that three ingredients differentiate it from other kinds (Leadbeater and Goss 1998). First, it is as much about political renewal as it is about managerial change, meaning public organisations renewing their sense of purpose, which is largely a political process. Second, from a leadership perspective civic entrepreneurship is essentially about collaborative leadership, working across boundaries and beyond organisations. Third, it is more than individual acts of innovation. It is about creating new services and products and exploiting maximum social value from them.

Motivation

In the public sector it has long been argued that leaders are differentiated from their private sector counterparts by the dimension of the public interest and that this altruism acts as a powerful motivator, particularly among professional staff such as those in health care. However, during the last 20 years most models for health care reform have been adopted from the business-based private sector and consequently, the challenge for health care leaders has been to merge that approach with the public service ethos of the service sector to create new forms of public leadership and organisational cultures.

Stability

Historically, public organisations have been seen as stable and less sensitive to environmental changes with the possible exception of the impact of political change. However, Chapter 3 presents a picture of significant reform and change either being implemented or being planned across Europe's health care systems. It may be the case that public bureaucracies are seldom completely abolished and public leaders seldom replaced but the leadership challenge for health care leaders of implementing major programmes of reforms is not to be underestimated; a challenge that is heightened in those countries where politicians have a direct impact on managerial appointments, for example Italy and Finland.

Power

This remains a significant leadership variable when comparing the two sectors. Public service leaders have to combine a number of skills in order to maintain a powerful position. First, they have to be able to relate to politicians because it is often they who determine policy, resources and timescales for action. Second, they have to respond to increasingly strong representation from consumers and patients' rights groups. And third, they have to operate at the interface between politicians, consumers and professional health care staff, successfully leading the latter in positive change. Although there are parallel forces in the private sector, the emergence of shareholder power in recent years for example, the strong political involvement in public services necessitates careful consideration by leaders of how power is exercised and maintained.

CONCLUSION

For a subject that has been so extensively researched it may be surprising that the above theories and models do not add up to any meaningful conclusion about the nature of leadership. What they clearly do is emphasise the peripheral elements of leadership such as traits, styles, preferred behaviours, contingencies, situation and effectiveness. The result has been the inability of academics to develop a school of leadership that clearly and consistently articulates an understanding of what leadership actually is. It is no wonder that leadership defies ambiguous definition. One of the problems is that leadership research has tended to be unidisciplinary in approach, for example social psychology or political science or sociology. Of particular importance to health and health care, with success increasingly dependent on networks, systems and inter-agency working, is that the majority of leadership research has been undertaken within organisations. Consequentially, there is a dearth of understanding of inter-organisational or network-based leadership. This is pursued further in Chapter 4, which discusses networks, partnerships and collaboration.

Future research needs to develop leadership as a strong inter-disciplinary area of study in its own right rather than as a sub-set of other academic disciplines. In particular, there is the need to develop future research that is grounded in what is real, what actually happens when leaders and followers engage in leadership. Future leadership research will be more effective when studies include academics and practitioners working together – or perhaps exchanging roles – to understand how leadership works in reality. Such collaboration is likely to be the only way to determine and record how leadership actually occurs both within and between organisations and across networks. With that kind of approach, leadership researchers have a much better chance of developing grounded conceptual frameworks that make sense and inform the practice of leadership in the future. In spite of these caveats, practical sense can be derived from the history of research on leadership styles. For the busy practising manager and aspiring leader the leadership literature can be distilled into four basic styles, as follows:

1   Autocratic

As its name suggests, this is the 'do-as-I-say' style. It is best avoided if your desire is to increase productivity, efficiency or staff commitment. However, the autocratic style does have its place, for example when dealing with indifferent or difficult staff, or when very firm and clear leadership is required such as during an emergency situation or crisis. It is difficult, for example, to imagine a surgeon behaving in any way other than autocratic during an emergency in the operating room. In addition, responding to organisational financial or operational crises can require autocratic leadership at times.

2   Democratic

This style has an emphasis on teamwork and should deliver all-round benefits. The style offers the opportunity for followers to voice their ideas and perspectives, and to take ownership of service and organisational objectives. The potential benefit of the democratic style of leadership is greater efficiency, staff commitment, increased job satisfaction and productivity.

3   Laissez-faire

As the name suggests, this is the 'hands-off' style of leadership. It is most effective when leading highly trained or professional staff dedicated to their work, such as those found in clinical services.

4   Situational leadership

As discussed on page 31 this style is dictated principally by the situation. For example, if your normal style of leadership is democratic but an unexpected and very tight deadline or crisis is looming, you might decide to take complete control and use an autocratic style until the event has passed.

DISCUSSION QUESTIONS

1 Are you aware of your dominant or preferred leadership style and the style that you revert to when under pressure?

2 Are there significant differences between your two leadership styles and are there aspects of either style that you think it would be helpful to change to make them more effective?

3 Can you identify situations in your organisation or service when different leadership models or styles have been required to produce the required outcome? How could these situations have been handled differently do you think?

4 Can you identify from your experience an example of an autocratic, democratic, laissez-faire and situational leader? What do you consider to be the strengths and weaknesses of their approaches and what can you personally learn from them?

BIBLIOGRAPHY AND FURTHER READING

Bass B.M. (1985) *Leadership and Performance Beyond Expectations*. New York: Free Press.

Bass B.M. (1990) *Bass and Stogdill's Handbook of Leadership Theory, Research and Managerial Applications*. New York: The Free Press.

Burns J.M. (1979) *Leadership*. New York: Harper & Row.

Collins J. (2001) *Good to Great*. New York: HarperCollins.

Conger J.A. and Kanungo R.N. (1998) *Charismatic Leadership in Organisations*. London: Sage.

Dawson S. (1996) *Analysing Organisations*. Basingstoke: Palgrave.

Kellerman B. (2004) *Bad Leadership: what it is, how it happens, why it matters*. Boston: Harvard Business School Press.

Lane J-E. (2000) *The Public Sector*, 3rd edn. London: Sage.

Leadbeater C. and Goss S. (1998) *Civic Entrepreneurship*. London: Demos.

Northouse P.G. (2001) *Leadership Theory and Practice*, 2nd edn. London: Sage.

Rost J.C. (1993) *Leadership for the Twenty-First Century*. London: Praeger.

Waldman D.A., Ramirez G.G., House R.J. and Puranam P. (2001) Does leadership matter? CEO leadership attributes and profitability under conditions of perceived environmental uncertainty. *Academy of Management Journal* 44(1): 134–143.

Yukl G. (1994) *Leadership in Organisations*. New Jersey: Prentice-Hall.

Chapter 3

The context of European health care

KEY POINTS OF THIS CHAPTER

■ Differences between the funding systems of health services in European countries have become less significant as a result of health service reforms in recent years.

■ There are quantitative differences between Europe's health care services but they all face pressure from the need for greater efficiency, the impact of increasing patient consumerism and worsening population health.

■ Structurally, there is a trend towards devolution of power and decentralisation in health sector reform.

■ There is emerging internationalisation of health care provision.

■ National governments directly influence the role of the local health care leader by determining policy, structure and organisational accountabilities and an important responsibility of the local leader is making sense of this national operating context.

■ Political will and leadership is the key to implementing health service reforms.

■ A key feature of professional organisations such as those in health care is that doctors, nurses and other clinical staff can exercise considerable power.

■ The risk for the health care leader is becoming squeezed between politically driven reform and resistance to change from the professional staff required to implement change.

KEY TERMS

- Europe and the European Union
- Consumer
- Context and environment
- Clinical leadership
- Reform and change
- Health care organisations, networks and services

INTRODUCTION

This chapter builds on the theme of context that emerged in Chapters 1 and 2 and discusses the working environment or context for leaders of health care organisations and clinical services. This chapter does not provide a detailed commentary on Europe's systems of health care but inter-country comparisons are made in order to draw out contextual similarities and differences. Reference is also made to the relevant public sector management literature, which has been influential in describing the contextual pressures faced by managers in public services. Like leadership itself, the environment cannot be precisely defined and it is best to think of it as a concept that embraces everything outside the organisation. It is a collection of views of individuals, groups and other organisations that share links with the organisation or service concerned. From a network perspective, an organisation's environment is a network of other organisations within which the environment consists of a field of relationships that bind organisations together (network and networking are discussed further in Chapter 4). For health care leaders, managing an organisation's environment and the relationships both within and beyond the organisation is important to organisational and personal success.

In their report on improving efficiency in European health care Wigdahl and Tomqvist (2004) comment that efficiency in the delivery of health care is a matter not solely for the health care sector but also for governments and commercial organisations. The challenges facing hospitals and other providers of health care across Europe stem from the macro-economic health changes occurring in most countries. Against that backdrop, whether health care providers are in competition with each other or under pressure from governments, the result is still the same: there is the need to dramatically improve the efficiency of health care delivery. One of the significant challenges is controlling expenditure and costs. Whereas governments' expenditure on health care as a percentage of GDP is between 7 and 12 per cent, the annual real increase in health spend has been between 3 and 5.5 per cent, which perhaps is not surprising for a sector that is more supplier led than most. Consequently, governments and insurers want to see a greater return on their expenditure. One example of the importance attached to health care costs by the commercial sector is General Motors, which spends over $2 billion per year on health care. The amount is routinely mentioned in assessments of the company's performance (Wigdahl and Tomqvist ibid.).

THE CONTEXT OF EUROPE'S HEALTH SERVICES

The European Union

In 2004 the European Union (EU) had its fifth and largest enlargement with ten new member states bringing the total membership to 25 states. Another three states are likely to follow in 2007. This makes the EU the largest politically and economically integrated transnational bloc in the world. However, after the June 2004 European elections, most of the EU's 15 old member states suffered from disgruntled voters taking the opportunity to punish their elected leaders. The results included a healthy dose of Euro-scepticism and were a disaster for the existing coalitions in many countries with the notable exceptions of Spain and Greece, which had only recently elected new national governments. However, the uncertainty generated by the 2004 election did not prevent the European Council agreeing the text of a proposed constitutional treaty, which was signed on 29 October 2004 in Rome. However, the rejection of the treaty by the French and Dutch in early 2005 reflects growing scepticism about the EU's role and expansion. The situation is made more uncertain by the wavering British commitment to a referendum, and the likelihood of new French and German leaderships in their next elections. Given this picture, attempts to extent the boundaries of European health policy are unlikely to be successful in the near future.

There is no EU health policy, partly because the EU has no formal role in health care services. Health care systems are subject to the subsidiarity principle and the preserve of national governments. However, this is unlikely to prevent the EU commenting on health care provision because the countries of Europe are increasingly being drawn together by two important issues: first, the movement of citizens between countries for health care treatment, a reflection of the growing importance of health consumerism; and second, the emergence of a common set of challenges to improve population health across most countries. The EU accepts the need for a permanent mechanism to support European cooperation in the field of health care, to monitor the impact of the

EU on health systems and to coordinate and manage the various discussions on health policy that are taking place under the umbrella of the EU. In July 2004 the European Commission proposed key principles to guide the development of EU policy, including the context of good health being a driver of economic growth and a shift from treating ill health to proactively promoting good health. The EU may be seen as a challenge for health services because it adds a further complexity to a number of contextual driving forces such as changing health care needs, increasing consumer expectation, the development of e-health and the regionalisation of political decision-making against the backdrop of economic globalisation (Busse *et al.* 2002).

At the first EU open health forum in Brussels on 17 May 2004, EU commissioners David Byrne and Pavel Telicka (2004) spoke on the future direction of EU health policy. They argued that the EU could function as a catalyst for change and facilitate progress against some major health policy achievements at a European level in recent years. Examples include progress on tobacco use, blood safety, and a planned European centre on disease prevention and control. The European-wide issues needing to be addressed reflect the health challenges of Europe's constituent countries, namely chronic diseases, ageing population, rising expectation from consumerism and the health gap between the ten new member states and the rest of the Union. The commissioners argue that there are four distinct areas where the EU can make a tangible contribution to improving the health of Europe's citizens:

- the provision of reliable information to promote active citizen participation in health decision-making processes;
- promoting health as a driver of economic growth;
- improving cooperation to ensure resources are used effectively;
- development of the EU role in international forums.

In 2004 a high-level group on health services and medical care was established, made up of representatives of the ministries of health of the 25 member states. The group has been charged with developing policy and initiatives to move forward on patient mobility. The European Court of Justice (ECJ) began taking an interest in patient mobility in 1998 because two Luxembourg citizens demanded reimbursement from their health insurance funds for treatment of their children in Belgium and Germany respectively. Although the Luxembourg health insurance companies did not see themselves under any obligation to reimburse the expenses, this was overturned by the ECJ because the citizens had invoked free movement of goods and services in the EU. This, the first of a number of rulings in this area, has made clear the impact that the single European market has on health services of EU member states. However, even if the impact of EU and ECJ interventions appears small, for example in terms of numbers of patients, the potential turbulence caused by these interventions is likely to be much greater. This could include the development of more competition in the provision of health care services; and patients could be reimbursed for health care services provided in another member state at the rate and tariff of their home member state only. The EU could also influence social security systems, which EU member states believe they have the power to structure without outside interference. In considering plans to reform the Netherland's system of health insurance because of financial challenges, van der Grinten and de Lint (2004) comment that legal precedents set by the ECJ could impact on social security systems, which may have implications for linked related health insurance systems.

The movement of patients could also be helped by consolidation of provision across countries and the slowly emerging internationalisation of health care provision. One example is the company Capio, which is now running hospitals in Sweden, Norway and the UK (Dixon-Fyle *et al.* 2004; Wigdahl and Tomqvist 2004). One policy that is having a more significant impact on the organisation of health services is the 1993 European Working Time Directive (EWTD), which protects the health and safety of workers by laying down minimum requirements in relation to working hours, rest periods, annual leave and working arrangements for night workers. A five-year transition period for the working pattern of doctors in training, ending in 2009, is currently being followed. Again, the ECJ has ruled on this issue. The first involved a Spanish primary-care facility taken in 1998; the second involving a German hospital doctor in 2002. These rulings impact on how the Directive is interpreted; for example in the case of the Spanish judgement, the ruling declared that all time spent resident on-call would count as working time. Perhaps the biggest impact of the EWTD is in Ireland, where it has triggered the most fundamental reform of the country's health care system for 50 years, largely because the country's small county hospitals could not possibly be staffed to meet EWTD standards. Whether a similar impact will be seen in other countries has yet to be seen.

Finally, the anticipated EU directive on recognition of professional qualifications has implications for workforce planning across the EU. The recognition will facilitate cross-border movement of health care professionals. This could result in workforce shortages in some countries, perhaps resulting in the use of staff from beyond Europe, such as suitably qualified refugees. In assessing possible scenarios for the future role and impact of the EU, Wismar and Busse (2002) conclude that only regulated competition would give Europe a definite role in health care. In this scenario, a convergence of organisations would occur over time led by the most successful. However, this would create a paradox because although health care is an economic burden in terms of state expenditure, it is also an asset in terms of employment and economic regeneration and an important link for other industries such as e-business and pharmaceuticals. In the light of these industrial interrelationships, it is difficult to imagine health care not playing a significant role in European integration.

Funding and organisation of health care

The systems of funding health services across Europe provide for universal or near universal coverage through either general taxation or contributions to health insurance funds. In most countries health care is financed through some combination of the following: general taxation from direct and indirect tax receipts; social insurance from employee and employer contributions; out-of-pocket payments made directly by patients; and private insurance taken out by individuals or employers. However, the differences between the funding systems have become less significant as a result of health care reforms in recent years. A UK government-commissioned review assessed the alternatives for the financing of health care taking into account detailed assessments from the academic literature (Wanless 2001). Of the 13 major countries studied, the UK was found to have the most progressive financing system overall. The review concluded that financing through general taxation is regarded as being more efficient than other means because it ensures strong cost control and prioritisation, better health outcomes and minimises economic distortions and disincentives. Importantly, the general taxation approach ensures the maximum separation between individual financial contributions and utilisation of health services, thereby ensuring the provision of universal access to health care irrespective of the ability to pay. This lack of discouragement from seeking treatment is also underscored by the general absence of out-of-pocket payments for services and treatment.

It is tempting when looking across Europe's health systems to make quantitative comparisons but this is not always helpful (Saltman and Figueras 1997). Consider the following. In 1994 the highest-spending country in Western Europe was Switzerland, which spends some six times more dollars per capita in absolute terms than Poland and also has an expenditure more than four times that of Greece and ten times that of Turkey, which hopes to join the EU in 2007. Austria, France and Germany each spend roughly one third above the Western European average of health care expenditure per head of population; Italy has three times more practising doctors per head of population than the UK; Germany has nearly twice as many nurses as Italy, Poland, Spain and the UK; while the number of hospital beds range from 17.9 per thousand population in Switzerland to 3.6 in Sweden (accepting that beds may be defined differently in different countries). Switzerland has the highest number of doctor contacts in Western Europe at 11 contacts per person in 1997 above the European average of 7.4 contacts per person. Such comparisons may look superficially attractive but are not particularly helpful in making incisive comparisons because they merely generate further questions and meaningful conclusions cannot always be drawn. Europe is not homogenous and each country has its own cultural, socio-economic and political history, much of which is undergoing change in many countries, particularly in Eastern Europe from the late 1980s onwards. For example, Slovenia underwent considerable socio-economic and political change in the period 1988 to 1991 with parliamentary democracy established in 1990, followed by independence in 1991. Changes like these will often have a major impact on the organisation and funding of health services. Slovenia introduced a health insurance system with universal coverage in 1992, along with the private provision of health care and the establishment of a chambers system for health professionals.

Further differences emerge when comparing health care practices; for example, in Sweden more care is provided outside hospital where the average length of stay in hospital is only five days, as compared to nearly ten days in Germany. Variations in the range of out-of-pocket spending are significant, with Italian patients making financial contributions to their health care at more than ten times the rate of UK patients. Closer inspection of the organisation of health services shows that the balance between primary and secondary care also varies with different degrees of freedom of choice for patients about who they can consult. Many patients across Europe are now expected to register with general practitioners or other physicians working in primary care and use them for their initial care. Most countries are turning to the view that gate-keeping or managed care systems are generally seen to be more efficient and countries lacking these systems are attempting to introduce them in response to various pressures. Poland recently introduced a gate-keeping system while in Germany attempts are being made to strengthen primary care with gate-keeping systems being introduced by some sickness funds. A key feature of the German health care delivery system is the clear institutional boundaries between the publicly provided health services, and ambulatory care through office-based physicians. Although Switzerland has a similar system, it has seen few major reforms because the referenda-driven political system makes comprehensive reform laws difficult to pass. However, managed care systems are being introduced in an attempt to control spending on ambulatory care and pharmaceuticals.

The French, German and Swiss systems currently contrast markedly with those of the Netherlands and the UK where primary care is regarded as an important priority. In the Netherlands the country's 7,000 general practitioners play a key role in providing most of the primary medical care and acting as gate-keepers to specialist services (Jacobs and Goddard 2000). All hospitals are owned and operated on a non-profit basis by private, locally controlled inde-pendent boards and very few acute hospitals are public. The hospital system is well developed comprising a network of general, single-specialty acute and university hospitals. A wide range of community facilities complements mental health hospital services. Most hospital investment is private and hospitals usually borrow from a banking system to finance acquisitions. The Netherlands is now also following Denmark and the UK in introducing a national system for blame-free reporting of medical errors.

The UK's taxation-based system is also undergoing governmental-driven change to improve efficiency and the experience of patients. The current health policy agenda, which has been strongly target-based in recent years, includes faster access to services, an increased emphasis on greater use of primary care, the further integration of health and social care, greater patient involvement and extended roles for health professionals. For example, advanced nurse practitioner-led 'walk in' centres have been introduced aimed at providing more flexible access and relieving the pressure on hospital emergency depart-ments from patients attending with non-urgent or primary care medical problems. There has also been the development of advanced practitioners and consultants in nursing and the therapy professions, partly to overcome the UK's medical workforce shortages. Greater use of the private and overseas independent sectors has been introduced to dramatically reduce waiting times for access to direct-treatment services. This is now being extended to diagnostic services, which historically have experienced long waiting times for MR and CT scanning. However, there are indications that the English government remains frustrated with the pace of change in the state system. To stimulate more rapid change the government announced in 2004 that futher waves of elective (namely non-urgent) patient treatment are to be undertaken by the independent sector.

MOBILITY AND CONSUMERISM

The importance of patient mobility is reflected by three developments. First, there is movement of patients between countries for treatment. In recent years UK patients who have been unable to secure treatment within a reasonable period are able to travel overseas to obtain it, including travelling to mainland Europe. For example, long waiting lists for IVF, coupled with changes to the

UK law in 2005 about the disclosure of egg and sperm donors, are forcing infertile couples to look abroad. Couples seeking some of the cheapest and most successful fertility treatments in Europe may soon be flying to Slovenia. It seems that the prospect of 'reverse health tourism' where UK couples travel to Eastern Europe for fertility treatment is likely. Second, as stated above, the ECJ has ruled that it is reasonable for patients to receive treatment without undue delay and they should be reimbursed by their own country under existing treaty provisions governing the free movement of goods and services. Third, a 2004 survey of 8,000 Europeans found that people would travel to another country for treatment if their own health system paid (Disney *et al.* 2004). The survey found that three-quarters of younger people would be willing to travel; and only older people in France and Germany were hesitant about travelling abroad for treatment.

Patients willing to travel for treatment are a reflection of the increasing importance of consumerism in European health care. In their book, *The European Patient of the Future*, Coulter and Magee (2003) identify a number of key issues for European patients based on consumer research across eight European countries. They found that the similarities were often more striking than the differences. The most common complaints were waiting times and access arrangements. This was followed by concerns about communication with health professionals, access to health information, continuity of care, involvement in decisions, choice of providers and an equitable system for accessing health care resources according to need. It also seems that most people are keen to take more responsibility for managing their own health care. European patients tend to react conservatively to suggestions that professional roles might change, for example the introduction of non-medical professionals with extended roles, but they do accept these changes when they see them occurring.

Europe's population health

The health challenges of countries across Europe are converging and are the result of demographic, lifestyle and environmental changes. People are living longer and there appears to be no limit to what can be done to keep people alive. New pharmacological developments such as antibiotics and immunosuppressive drugs appear every year along with developments in organ transplantation, joint replacements and overall life support. Population health is generating similar challenges. It is estimated that between 20–30 per cent of adults in Europe are overweight because of poor diet and lack of physical activity. Cardiovascular disease is now responsible for 40 per cent of all deaths (Byrne 2003).

The future of children's health does not look too bright either. In 2004 the World Health Organisation (WHO) published the largest ever survey of the lifestyles of 160,000 school children in 35 countries across Europe, Canada and the USA (WHO 2004). The report provides damning evidence that dietary and lifestyle problems beset a number of countries. It was found that one in four 15-year-olds smoke weekly while 19 per cent said that they had used cannabis in the previous 12 months. The percentage of 15-year-old girls who said that they had had sexual intercourse varied greatly across the countries surveyed, from ten per cent in Poland, Greece and Israel, to more than 40 per cent in Wales, England and Greenland. Other indicators of youth health examined included physical activity, bullying and fighting and communication with parents. The report also describes the social and economic circumstances of young peoples' lives, including their family situations. In publishing the report, WHO called for more action from governments, civil society, international agencies, and parents and young people.

The health of the people of Europe represents a major challenge for public health not only in tackling the state of population health but also incorporating public health principles in the reform of health care services. In the light of the socio-economic situation facing most countries, increasing the capacity of health care provision to treat increasing numbers of sick people is neither a sustainable nor affordable strategy. Reforming health care provision and tackling societal issues that contribute to poor health is. The key policy areas for stimulating good health are education, housing, economic generation, transport, employment, environment and recreational facilities. It is action in these areas that will have a much greater impact on levels of physical and mental health. Good public health, most commonly defined as the promotion of health and prevention of disease through the organised effort of society (WHO 1996), is most effectively pursued on a cross-governmental and inter-agency basis. And effective health promotion requires a move from policies based on education to those that help individuals to make healthy choices, whether by empowering them through advocacy or community development. To give one example, in the UK local (municipal) authorities have been required since 2000 to produce a community strategy to promote the economic, social and environmental well-being of their communities. They are required to bring together the public, private, voluntary and community sectors to provide a single, overarching, local coordination framework within which other, more specific, local partnerships can operate. Of course, governments can go further to improve population health by also introducing regulation. However, only two countries, Ireland and Norway, have implemented a ban on smoking in public places; and only two additional countries, Scotland and England, have announced that a similar ban will be introduced in the next few years.

Links between health and health care have also been explored in England. Following the Labour government's commitment to bring health spending up to the EU average, it also investigated future funding needs in the context of NHS spending having grown by an average of 3.6 per cent a year in real terms since the 1970s, but nevertheless falling behind other EU countries. A faster rate of increase was recommended but with the warning that seven per cent a year real growth in spending was at the upper end of what could be spent efficiently by the NHS (Wanless 2002). Nevertheless the Government adopted this figure, which will increase NHS spending by £90 billion by 2007–08, an increase of 44 per cent in real terms from the point at which the big expansion started in 2002. However, reform is also planned including a greater emphasis on prevention and public health. A subsequent report made recommendations for reducing the illnesses and diseases of today's modern Western lifestyle such as obesity (Wanless 2004). A scenario for the UK NHS in 2022 was recommended in which levels of public engagement in relation to their health are high; life expectancy increases go beyond current forecasts; health status improves dramatically; and people are confident in what by then will be a more efficient, consumer responsive and quality-led health system.

Public health services also have an important role in evaluating the effectiveness of health services and in designing and implementing mechanisms to make services more appropriate, efficient and equitable in provision. The WHO argues that the reform of health services provides an opportunity to strengthen public health infrastructure across all sectors of society; to define national policy and priorities linked not only to health care but to determine use of health and health gain; to improve health promotion and inter-sectoral strategies; and to re-orientate the public health service to support the health care services in pursuit of health gain. To achieve all that requires health professionals to assess the health needs of populations and to then design, implement and evaluate appropriate strategies and tactics in response to those needs against the backdrop of ongoing reform of public and health care services. This represents an enormous challenge and considerably enhanced professional and personal skills.

CLINICAL LEADERSHIP

At a national level there is evidence that the influence of the medical profession on health policy is declining in the industrialised countries of Europe (Raffel 1997). This is partly because of health service cost pressures on other parts of national economies such as from the medical devices and pharmaceutical industries. Costs are also generated by the actions of doctors themselves, and the impact of rising costs on the national economy results in governments and other stakeholders, such as business leaders, becoming more vocal about the future organisation of health care systems in the context of choice over future national economic investment. The situation is different of course within the micro-world of the health care organisation where a key feature of these professional organisations is that doctors, nurses and other clinical staff can exercise considerable power. Consequently, they have a large degree of control across organisations, and often beyond, as a result of professional networks. As a result, the ability of health care leaders to determine and secure agreement to objectives for change and influence decision-making is far more constrained and contingent than in other organisations. Hospitals and other health care organisations have an inverted power structure, in which people at the bottom generally have greater influence over decision-making on a day-to-day basis than those who are nominally in control at the top.

At the heart of the issue is the tension between doctors and managers, which is summarised as doctors wanting to do the greatest good for the individual and managers wanting to do the greatest good for the greatest number of people. Both managers and doctors will commit resources and exercise judgement in doing so. However, managers will be working through others to ensure that whole organisations or services work smoothly while clinical professionals will exercise judgement about individual patients. The tension is most often seen when health care managers and leaders attempt to secure clinician agreement to cost- and efficiency-driven objectives such as the prescribing of generic rather than branded drugs; the introduction of standardised diagnostic and treatment protocols; and improving efficiency, for example by greater use of day-care treatment rather than patients staying overnight. Inpatient care typically consumes 45–75 per cent of health care resources and across Europe there is an increasing belief that there are more cost-effective alternatives (WHO 1996). Further, since publication of the 2000 World Health Report (WHO 2000), comparisons of health system performance are now on the international policy agenda (Nolte and McKee 2003). Considerable interpersonal and influencing skills are often required by managers to secure clinician agreement to change in an area that is still seen by much of the medical profession as their sole preserve. Consequently, in the disconnected hierarchy of the health care organisation or local health system, organisational leaders have to negotiate rather than impose new policies and practices (Ham 2003). Failure to recognise this fact and carry doctors and other clinical professionals along with change will invariably result in the mixed implementation of reform. Consequently, ways have to be found of generating change bottom up, not just top down, by engaging health care professionals in reform processes such as working groups, task-forces and by giving them leadership roles and responsibilities so they feel they are leading the process instead of having it imposed upon them. Leaders of health care organisations and services also need to recognise the importance of collegiate working in medicine and influences in professional organisations and the impact that external, regulatory organisations have on professional practice.

There are two obstacles to engaging clinical staff effectively in the development of clinical leadership. The first is to be found in the nature of professional work in health care. Autonomy remains highly valued and there is reluctance on the part of some doctors to lend support to their peers who take on management and leadership roles. The second obstacle to progress is the impatience of reformers such as politicians whose time horizons are largely determined by electoral cycles and the need to satisfy their electorates. Consequently, changes in health system performance and clinical engagement are probably best achieved by a series of incremental steps rather than through step change but this is unlikely to satisfy politicians who increasingly expect to see quick results. The result will be a widening gulf of understanding between politicians and leaders of health care organisations, and also between those leaders and clinical professionals.

LEADERSHIP IN A POLITICAL ENVIRONMENT

The role of the state

In the late 1980s many European governments began to re-examine the structure of governance in their health care systems (Saltman and Figueras ibid.; WHO 1996). In particular, the role of the state as being the central player in health care is being reassessed. National policy-makers of many countries have felt compelled by a combination of economic, social, demographic, managerial, technological and ideological forces to review existing authority relationships and structures. Europe seems to have experienced a widespread disillusionment with large, centralised and bureaucratic institutions and in almost every country, whether economically developed or not, the same drawbacks of centralised systems are being identified: low levels of efficiency, slow pace of change and innovation, and the lack of essential environmental and socio-economic changes to improve population health. As a consequence, the structural reform themes that now link countries across Europe are decentralisation and devolution of power. In the context of historical public sector management research, the extent to which the management of health services is devolved is an important factor in developing local leadership capacity and capability. Decentralisation and devolvement of authority is seen as an effective means to:

■ stimulate improvements in service delivery by motivating local leaders and clinical staff;
■ secure the better use of resources according to needs;
■ help reduce inequities in health;
■ involve local populations in decisions about priorities and health care services.

The result has been that some state functions have been devolved to regional and municipal authorities. For example, Spain's programme of decentralising its health service started in the 1980s and resulted in ending the historically highly centralised, national model of health care administration. Models in each region vary but the governments of the autonomous communities are responsible for the management of the health services to their regional parliaments, which determine the regional health care budgets. Some regions have their own health plans and it has not proved possible to institute an integrated national health plan except in certain key areas. Two key elements of recent reforms, focusing on promoting equal access to health services by correcting structural inequalities, were the establishment of stable teams of medical professionals working full-time in primary health care centres and the building of new hospitals in rural areas to reverse the geographical inequalities generated during the Franco era. With the exception of certain regions, the main hospitals in Spain are owned by central or regional government and are university affiliated and publicly funded. In some regions there is a mix of private and public funding. However, ten years after the reforms their impact on the organisation and managerial modernisation of the system was not evident (Saltman and Figueras 1997).

At the same time as accelerating the decentralisation of administrative responsibility, most countries are in the process of establishing or strengthening national bodies to take responsibility for overseeing professional training, regulation and quality assurance. Some governments have also sought to apply private sector management practices to public sector organisations. Known as the new public management, this strategy emphasises the importance of competition and performance management although some critics would argue that this results in a proliferation of managers and erodes the so-called public service ethos (Dawson and Dargie 2002). Although the 'how' of responding to these challenges may be in dispute, the 'what' of the challenges are not: health and health care are becoming ever more challenging, complex environments, necessitating the need for more effective management and associated systems. In short, the countries of Europe not only have similar problems but are addressing them in similar ways. To take another example, Finland operates with a municipal-based structure. The country's health care system is financed mainly by taxation with most health services provided by public service providers. The central government's role is to plan, supervise and finance about 50 per cent of services. The municipalities are self-governing, with democratically elected representation and they have the right to levy local taxes. Finland's reform of giving the municipalities more freedom and responsibility to organise their services with the minimum of directives from government is aimed at pushing back the frontiers of public regulation and controlling spending by generating competition, cost containment and innovation.

Decentralisation may be as easy to achieve, as it appears to be in Finland, but by itself may not be sufficient as two examples of limited progress show. Poland and Hungary embarked on a process to strengthen authorities at local level, whose influence on health matters had been very limited (Saltman and Figueras ibid.). A pilot project in Poland in 1994 is an example of cautious devolution. Decision-making power for health services was transferred to local authorities in 28 cities where more than 20 per cent of the country's population reside. Success in Hungary has been more limited. The self-regulating health insurance system and the establishment of an independent health insurance fund were major achievements in the country's decentralisation process. However, although decentralisation and regionalisation were strongly emphasised by the government's 1994 reform programme, implementation was never begun and structurally, the government's approach to the reorganisation of hospital services continues to favour centralisation.

What the above health policies and reforms show is the importance and impact of the national political and macro-economic context on the structure, organisation and provision of local health services. Almost irrespective of the funding arrangements for health services, national governments directly influence the role of the local health care leader by determining policy, structure and organisational accountabilities of the health care bodies they create. The structure of a country's political institutions can have a major impact on its ability to achieve health sector reform. For example, England's central government has forced through major, national structural reform while Sweden, with its regionally based government structure, has been more adept at testing a variety of different reforms through demonstration and pilot projects. The Swedish regional county councils, together with central government, form the basis of the health care system with its three political levels of national, regional and local. Most health care facilities and hospitals are owned and operated by the county councils, although in Stockholm more than 50 per cent of primary care is now available from privately organised providers procured by the county council.

In countries with multi-party coalitions, such as the Netherlands, or where there is a second national legislative body, for example in Germany, reform tends to be incremental because of the need for it to be politically negotiated. After reunification, German hospitals were faced with a rapidly changing environment of fixed budgets and the possibility of deficits. As a result, the hospital sector, which concentrates on inpatient care only, is much less stable and by international comparison, admissions to hospital and length of stay are well above average. Treatment based on day cases is new for German hospitals, which have an average occupancy of 80 per cent (Jacobs and Goddard 2000). Pursuing reform can also be complicated by the relative strength of private interests in relation to public services such as the partially independent stake-holders that are involved. The history of these relationships influences the capacity of a national or regional government to introduce successful change. A Swedish government publication sums up well the attractions and potential pitfalls of importing reforms from other countries:

> The grass is definitely greener on our side, but let us get some seeds from our own neighbour to enrich the gene variation, seems to be the basic strategy. Countries tend basically to keep their cultural system heritage, but the growing need for 'urgent' solutions and the diffusion of ideas is increasingly followed by imports of methods from other systems. Evidently, the risks in such hasty imports is that you do not investigate enough the experience of the imported elements. You may cure the immediate problems, but bring other unwanted effects.
>
> (Olsson *et al.* 1993)

In addition to politics, contextual factors such as societal values influence the development of health care reform. But for any country the central constraint in implementing reform is the strength of its economy. Poorly performing national economies place greater pressure on public expenditure and in some countries this has resulted in attempts to shift financial burdens from central state bodies to individuals, autonomous institutions or regional and local authorities. In periods of economic retrenchment and reducing health budgets there is less flexibility and managers and clinical staff are not as posi-tively motivated, which means that greater leadership is required. Finally, external factors such as the transference of reform models and ideas across national boundaries also influence reform programmes. The UK NHS model influenced the creation of national health services in Greece, Italy, Portugal and Spain in the 1970s and 1980s. Importing reform models from other countries may well provide a quick, beneficial start and influence the formulation of new, home-grown reform programmes but in common with the management of change generally there are also significant implications for implementation. In some cases, the imported reforms may have little support from local health care leaders and clinical professionals because they are seen to have been imposed from outside with little opportunity for local influence over content. This is because national politicians often embrace new reform strategies for ideological reasons with little understanding of the local leadership, managerial skills, workforce or technical resources required to put them in place. Having said that, governmental political will and leadership have been identified as the most important factors affecting policy implementation (WHO 1996). While it is positive to learn about the health service reforms of other countries, perhaps even more so today when many face similar challenges, proper consideration of country-specific cultural and contextual issues is required before implementation.

In addition to importing reforms from outside the country, one of the greatest pressures for change has also been in the relative role of the private sector in operating and, in some countries, financing health care services (Saltman and Figueras 1997). Both place considerable pressure on local leaders and can hamper implementation of overall reform particularly when the country concerned has less-developed incumbent health systems. Turkey anticipates becoming an EU member soon, but it exemplifies the challenges of developing a health system in a developing country. The end of the 1990s saw over 100 new private hospitals established, mainly in the largest cities. However, the country's health care system faces problems of low population coverage, heavy reliance on out-of-pocket payments and an uneven distribution of facilities. All of this has led to an inadequate and unequal access to health services. Although a universal health insurance scheme has been an objective of every government health plan since 1963, universal coverage remains an elusive goal. There is an established network of primary care infrastructure throughout the country but the quality of services provided is variable. The distribution of secondary and tertiary health services is uneven and in urban areas they tend to be used for primary care purposes. One third of hospital beds and almost half of all doctors are concentrated in the three largest cities. Workforce issues are challenging; doctor and nurse to population ratios are comparatively low in Turkey with the skill-mix restricting the delivery of effective health services with too few nurses and midwives in relation to doctors, and until recently too many specialists in relation to general practitioners. Finally, reform attempts also have been hampered by political instability; for example, between 1993 and 1997 Turkey had six different ministers of health and consequentially, fragmented policy-making.

At the other end of the spectrum countries much more politically stable than Turkey are not immune from pressure for change. In recent years the WHO named the French health service as the best in the world (WHO 2000). Today, the system is falling deep into deficit and failing to cope with crises like the heat wave of 2003 (Jemiai 2004). Although patients have complete freedom to choose their doctors, the system is complex and costly. Hospital provision is generous and hospital care accounts for approximately half of total health care expenditure. Inpatient care is available from a choice of public and private hospitals. The former provide some three quarters of hospital beds and are considerably larger and better equipped than those in the private sector. The French system may be relatively equitable but it is inefficient and waiting lists for routine operations have begun to appear for the first time. In an attempt to stave off the collapse of the system, the 2004 government has promised radical reform. To reduce expenditure the government wants to end the right for the French to consult different doctors for the same complaint. In future, the first doctor to be consulted would become the case doctor and only they could recommend that a patient should seek a second or more specialist opinion. The political challenge is huge if only because the large majority of French people are broadly satisfied with their health service. They view the system positively even if it is expensive and none too efficient.

Switzerland is another example of a health care system built on long-term political stability. Like the country as a whole, the system is characterised by federalism and liberalism (Jacobs and Goddard 2000). Health care is mainly delivered by physicians in private practice and public hospitals where both inpatient and outpatient care is offered. Until relatively recently, state intervention at the federal level has traditionally been kept to a minimum and much of the responsibility for financing, organising and delivering health care has fallen to other players. The health insurance system is relatively decentralised although 1996 saw the federal law on sickness insurance revised to include the principle of universality and competition between the Swiss sickness funds as one of several measures aimed at containing costs.

All countries across Europe are pursuing reform and change of one form or another. While this is often challenging enough for those in leadership roles in the countries concerned, the leadership task is made more challenging in countries having to financially retrench compared to others whose health care services are expanding through investment. An important responsibility of the local health care leader is making sense for those around them of the national, external environment so that in turn, local aims and objectives can be determined and agreed. It has long been argued that there are key constraints on the strategic managerial behaviour and choices of public service managers compared to those in the private sector (Stewart *et al.* 1980; Ring and Perry 1985; Stewart *et al.* 1988; Dopson and Stewart 1989; Dawson *et al.* 1995). They concern the ambiguity of policy directives, the relative openness of decision-making, the greater number of influencing interest groups, the artificiality of time constraints and the relative instability of policy coalitions. Health care leaders of most if not all countries across Europe will recognise these constraints, many of which are likely to be in existence for some time given the socio-economic and political contexts of many countries. As a consequence of these constraints, the strategic management of public services may be extremely difficult, necessitating good political skills particularly when managers need to communicate with politicians, external stakeholders and patient pressure groups over which they have no authority. There are also additional differences in public service managerial attitudes to change (Dawson *et al.* ibid.):

- a tendency in the public services to criticise managerial mistakes;
- changes based on private sector practice seen as politically imposed and at odds with public service values;
- pursuing managerial agendas within a highly politicised context;
- working in the spotlight of intense media interest resulting in uncertainty, turbulence and intra-organisational defensiveness.

Other potential constraints for local leaders of health care organisations and systems include the ethos and history of local services, the availability of resources, the expectations of local players of the individual's leadership style and interference from the management tier above. Because of the often strong external controls exercised on public service bureaucracies through political processes or through lobbyists and pressure groups, high penalties can be exacted for failure. In some countries hospital chief executives are political appointments and subject to possible change whenever the government changes, for example in Italy. Italy's health system is a mixed, predominantly public one. Although there is a national public service the private sector covers almost all areas of medical care from general practice to specialist, hospital medicine and paramedical activities. Reforms in the 1990s transformed local health units into public enterprises with organisational autonomy and responsibility, managed by a general manager appointed by the regions on the basis of a contract renewable every five years. Larger hospitals can establish themselves as independent public hospital agencies with autonomous organisation and administration. They operate with balanced budgets and surpluses can be used for investment and staff incentives. Unjustified deficits can result in the loss of their autonomous status. However, the Italian health service appears to be marked by inequalities in provision round the country, with notable spending and contributory differences among the developed and less well-developed regions. In the politically driven environment of Italy's health system, leaders of health care will need to respond positively to political objectives for personal success and survival.

There are two potential adverse consequences of operating in politically driven environments. First, strong external control of organisations tends to lead to centralisation including strong central control inside organisations; and second, when the penalty for failure is higher for action than it is for inaction, it is often safer not to act than to act and be proven wrong. There is, however, evidence from the UK NHS of chief executives ignoring their constraints, exercising leadership and taking calculated, bold decisions with resultant organisational and personal success (Goodwin 2002). Half of the chief executives who formed the focus of the research were not constrained in their actions by either the national or local environment. The chief executives successfully established a local leadership culture by tackling significant local challenges in an inclusive way. They developed positive and influential interpersonal relationships with key players who were seen themselves as local leaders with their own networks of influential relationships. Paradoxically, because the chief executives were seen to take risks and act decisively, the result was an environment of relatively stable and cohesive interpersonal and inter-organisational relationships. These relationships were then used as the basis for further, successful change such as that flowing from nationally driven reform of health care. In addition, the chief executives had developed high-performing teams that they used to the full. The skills of individual team members complemented those of the chief executive who allowed each member to act as a leader in their own right when required. In short, the chief executives were comfortable with their role and not preoccupied with their own leadership image. They demonstrated personal maturity and humility, acting for the greater good of their organisations and wider health systems.

To be successful the effective leader of a health care organisation or system will need to devote greater energy to managing the interface between the organisation and the political process. The successful leader will devise a variety of strategies to somehow alter the situation confronting the organisation to make compliance less necessary. In other words, organisations and their leaders need to transact with elements of the environment in order to obtain the resources to survive. Figure 3.1 shows a simple four-way typology of

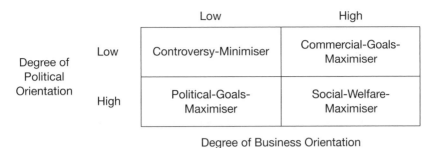

		Low	High
Degree of Political Orientation	Low	Controversy-Minimiser	Commercial-Goals-Maximiser
	High	Political-Goals-Maximiser	Social-Welfare-Maximiser

Degree of Business Orientation

Figure 3.1 *Chief executives of state-owned enterprises: a typology*

leadership styles for chief executives in state-owned enterprises. The typology, based on international research, shows how public service managers need to balance their political and managerial pressures in order to pursue leadership (Ramamurti 1987). Business orientation is the extent to which a manager is furthering the business objectives of a state-owned enterprise while political orientation is the extent to which that is being furthered. It is the social-welfare maximiser, the manager who scores high on both orientations, which is the ideal model to be aimed for because it combines the managerial strengths of the private sector with the non-economic welfare ethos of public services.

CONCLUSION

Leaders of health care organisations and health care systems across most European countries are facing almost unprecedented pressures. The history, structure and extent of centralised control of health care systems across Europe underscore the importance and influence of the context within which health care leaders and clinical professionals pursue their different roles in the provision and organisation of health care services. No country has the perfect health care system because each is being driven by differing socio-economic and political history and some countries are still consolidating their new political structures. Many governments are responding to increasing consumer demand by pursuing strategies to reduce access times for diagnostic testing and patient treatment, and demanding that providers of health care services offer high-quality services in line with international standards. Governments also are struggling to respond to the lack of incentives for patients and health care providers to restrain what they see as excessive utilisation of health care services, particularly hospitals. Against the backdrop of ageing populations across the countries of Europe these pressures are likely to increase before they can be stabilised by, among other things, the introduction of alternative and more cost-efficient forms of non-hospital based diagnosis and treatment coupled with greater use of self-care by people themselves.

There is a general discontent with current methods of financing and delivering health care and although governments see structural change as the solution to many of these ills it is by no means certain whether the numerous reform programmes across Europe will deliver the required results. The risk for the European Union is that it will fall into the trap of its constituent countries and become more involved in health care systems, ignoring the broader public health and health improvement agenda which would deliver benefits in the longer-term (Hunter 2003). In summary, countries are now facing a set of four pressures that will challenge not only the EU and national politicians but also the local leaders of practically all health care organisations and clinical professionals across virtually every country:

1   the drive for greater efficiency, productivity and cost control;
2   the growing demand for health care as a result of ageing populations and improvements in medical technology and pharmaceuticals;
3   the need to devise effective and sustainable responses to increasing consumer demands for greater patient choice, better and faster access to services, and the growing number of patients' rights movements;
4   the need to manage chronic diseases such as diabetes, heart disease and obesity, precipitated by increasing longevity, lifestyle and environmental changes.

However, caution is urged in thinking that successfully meeting these challenges is all that needs to be done. Few health care challenges are permanently met because of the dynamic and changing context of health care. Today's solutions will become tomorrow's new challenges as the history of developments in health care technology and pharmaceuticals show. Consequently, the process of reforming health services is continual as the experience of Europe's countries to date is demonstrating. It is not surprising that health care leaders have to regularly rethink their role against the backdrop of their ever-changing and complex world. Leaders of health care organisations are responsible for understanding national context and interpreting it in their local context with the objective of successfully engaging clinical leaders and other stakeholders in implementing reform and change. This is discussed further in Chapter 6 when the results of a major qualitative research study into chief executive health care leadership are presented. In the European-wide and national contexts facing today's health care leaders the real risk they face is being squeezed between the politicians driving the reforms and resistance from the very professional staff essential to implement change at a local level. High-performing leaders know that organisational and personal success is dependent on the development of a network of other leaders and followers, which is hard enough for any leader to achieve without the added complexity of doing so in a professionally based system such as health care. Never before has the need to understand context and manage the environment been more important for the European health care leader. To summarise, the personal challenge for health care leaders is, in common with the challenges facing them, also fourfold:

1   making sense of the context for reform and change so that the leader's team, wider stakeholders and clinical leaders can participate in the development of a vision for change;
2   developing a leadership team and a wider network of supporting leaders to take forward the changes for support and implementation;
3   within the leader's organisation or network, engaging clinical directors and clinical professional staff in the implementation process;
4   beyond the boundaries of the organisation, securing key stakeholder involvement from patients' groups, politicians and other clinical staff with professional links to the organisation.

These challenges move the discussion of the first three chapters from the 'how' to the 'what' of leadership and the process of how to develop personal and team leadership. These issues now constitute the remaining chapters of the book starting with Chapter 4, which is concerned with networks, partnership and collaboration.

DISCUSSION QUESTIONS

1   As a leader of a health care organisation, network or clinical service do you understand the national context within which you work in terms of the policies and the drivers for change?
2   Can you explain the national context to people around you in ways they will understand, explaining how the context will affect the future direction of the organisation, network or service?
3   Does your interpretation of the national context offer any opportunities for the development or positive change by motivating your organisation, network or service and others such as external stakeholders?

4   Does your interpretation or that of your organisation's offer any opportunities for the development or positive change that may help motivate people around you and other stakeholders?

5   Are you clear about who are the internal and external stakeholders whose support is required for any changes resulting from your interpretation of the impact of the national context? Can you map their likely responses and what they will look for in return for their support?

6   Have you reviewed the membership and skills of your immediate management team to ensure that you have the necessary support to respond positively to any changes arising from the national context?

BIBLIOGRAPHY AND FURTHER READING

Busse R., Wismar M. and Berman P.C. (eds) (2002) *The European Union and Health Services. The impact of the Single European Market on Member States.* Amsterdam: IOS Press.

Byrne D. (2003) Finding solutions. *Public Services Review: European Union* Autumn. Newcastle-under-Lyme: PSCA International.

Byrne D. and Telicka P. (2004) The future direction of health policy. *Eurohealth* 10(2): 4–5.

Coulter A. and Magee H. (2003) *The European Patient of the Future.* Berkshire: Open University Press.

Dawson S. and Dargie C. (2002) New Public Management: a discussion with special reference to the UK. In McLaughlin K., Osborne S.P. and Ferlie E. (eds) *New Public Management. Current trends and future prospects.* London: Routledge.

Dawson S., Winstanley D., Mole V. and Sherval J. (1995) *Managing in the NHS. A study of senior executives.* London: HMSO.

Disney H., Horn K., Hrobon P., Hjertqvist J., Kilmarnock A., Mihm A., Mingardi A., Philippe C., Smith D., van den Broek E. and Verhoeks G. (2004) *Impatient for Change. European attitudes to healthcare reform.* London: The Stockholm Network.

Dixon-Fyle S., Forn R., Henke N., Janus F. and Rizzuto C. (2004) Opportunities for internationalization in health care. *Health Europe. Management know-how for the health care industry,* 3, March: 74–85.

Dopson S. and Stewart R. (1989) *Widening the Debate of Public and Private Sector Management.* Management Research Paper. Oxford: Templeton College.

Goodwin N. (2002) *Determining the Leadership Role of Chief Executives in the English NHS.* Unpublished PhD thesis. Manchester Business School, University of Manchester.

Ham C. (2003) Improving the performance of health services: the role of clinical leadership. *The Lancet* 25 March: 1–3.

Hunter D.J. (2003) *Public Health Policy*. Cambridge, UK: Polity.

Jacobs R. and Goddard M. (2000) *Social Health Insurance Systems in European Countries. The role of the insurer in the health care system: a comparative study of four European countries*. York: Centre for Health Economics, The University of York.

Jemiai N. (2004) Recent French health system reform proposals. *Euro Observer* 6(2): 1–3.

Nolte E. and McKee M. (2003) Population health in Europe: how much is attributable to health care? *Euro Observer* 5(4): 1–3.

Olsson S.E., Hansen H. and Eriksson I. (1993) Social Security in Sweden and other European countries – three essays. *Finans-Departementet. Stockholm*: 150. Quoted in Raffel M.W. (ed.) (1997) *Health Care and Reform in Industrialized Countries*. Pennsylvania: The Pennsylvania State University Press, p. 303.

Raffel M.W. (ed.) (1997) *Health Care and Reform in Industrialized Countries*. Pennsylvania: The Pennsylvania State University Press.

Ramamurti R. (1987) Leadership styles in state-owned enterprises. *Journal of General Management* 13(2): 45–55.

Ring P.S. and Perry J.L. (1985) Strategic Management in Public and Private Organisations: implications of distinctive context and constraints. *Academy of Management Review* 10(2): 276–286.

Saltman B. and Figueras J. (eds) (1997) *European Health Care Reform*. Copenhagen: World Health Organisation.

Stewart R., Smith P., Blake J. and Wingate P. (1980) *The District Administrator in the National Health Service*. London: King Edward's Hospital Fund.

Stewart R., Gabbay J., Dopson S., Smith P. and Williams D. (1988) *Role and Progress of District General Managers: an overview*. Oxford: Templeton College.

Van der Grinton T.E.D. and de Lint M.W. (2004) Private health insurance, commercialisation and EU legislation. The next stage in Dutch health reform. *Eurohealth* 10(2): 26–30.

Wanless D. (2002) Securing our future health: taking a long-term view. London: HM Treasury, HMSO.

Wanless D. (2004) Securing good health for the whole population. Final Report. London: HM Treasury, HMSO.

Wigdahl N. and Tomqvist K. (2004) *Improving Efficiency in European Healthcare*. London: Report by Applied Value LLC.

Wismar M. and Busse R. (2002) Scenarios on the future of healthcare in Europe. In Busse R., Wismar M. and Berman P.C. (eds) (2002) *The European Union and Health Services. The impact of the Single European Market on Member States.* Amsterdam: IOS Press.

World Health Organization (1996) *European Health Care Reforms. Analysis of current strategies.* Copenhagen: WHO.

World Health Organization (2000) *The World Health Report. Health systems performance: Improving performance.* Geneva: WHO.

World Health Organization (2004) *Young People's Health in Context. Health Behaviour in School-Aged Children (HBSC) Study: international report from the 2001/2002 survey.* Copenhagen: WHO.

Chapter 4

Networks, partnerships and collaboration

KEY POINTS OF THIS CHAPTER

- The leadership process is common to both public and private sectors, and it is only the context that is different. However, there are few relevant studies focusing on leadership as a process.

- It is the successful management of significant local issues such as service and financial strategies by chief executives and their teams that creates a local leadership culture, which then forms a basis for further, successful change.

- Boundary crossing and creating inter-dependencies are important skills because health care cannot be organised nor controlled from one centre.

- The network organisation is a distinct structural form that is neither market nor hierarchy. Those who occupy central positions in a network and exercise control over the flow of information are most likely to emerge as leaders.

- For the more successful leaders, networking with outsiders including socialising and politicking, has a statistically significant relationship to personal managerial success.

- Collaborative advantage comes from work in large public sector organisations. It is concerned with the creation of synergy between collaborating organisations and their management teams.

- For collaboration to be successful stakeholder consideration must be at the heart of the leader's approach. Creating strong interpersonal relationships as the basis of effective inter-organisational collaboration requires trust as an absolute necessity.

■ Failing to manage upwards could have adverse consequences. The main aim of successful upward management is to achieve mutual trust and support.

KEY TERMS

■ Network and networking
■ Boundary crossing
■ Collaboration and collaborative advantage
■ Stakeholders
■ Managing upwards

INTRODUCTION

As illustrated in the last chapter, today's world of health management is complex, but the European and national contexts are converging into a common set of pressures for all health care leaders. The organisational or clinical service leader can achieve little without securing the active support and involvement of a network of influential individuals both inside and outside the organisation. The need for health care leaders to develop a stronger external leadership role is underscored by the growing influence of consumerism and the need to frequently explain changes in the local organisation of health care services to consumers, the public, politicians and patients' rights groups. This is as a result of developments in medical technology, pharmacology and patient treatment. The previous chapters have shown that successful leadership is dependent on understanding context and developing successful interpersonal and inter-organisational relationships in order to move forward with change. As such, leadership is not a series of single actions but a process of continual interaction with others in order to create networks of other leaders and followers who are prepared to support an implementation agenda for change.

Leadership is an interpersonal-based activity and consequentially, it is a process. Chapter 1 reminded us that today's generation of female and male leaders, compared to those of previous generations are more likely to be open to consensus building, participative decision-making, and delegation of responsibility and the empowerment of followers. The preoccupation of the last century with leadership tasks is now being replaced by an emphasis on people issues such as the mutuality and reciprocity of leader–follower relations. Today's leaders are likely to create and communicate a shared vision of the future that creates a common ground among people of differing views. In summary, leadership is essentially concerned with successfully implementing change by developing influential and empathetic interpersonal relationships in order to: create an agenda for change using a strong vision; and build a strong implementation network to get things done through other people. The previous chapters were concerned with explaining what leadership is, the context within which it is practised and the challenges arising from context. This chapter is concerned with the 'how' of leadership; specifically, how it is pursued by the development of interpersonal, inter-departmental and inter-organisational networks.

LEADERSHIP AS A PROCESS

The process by which leadership is pursued is the same for both the public and private sectors. It is only the context that is different and as the last chapter showed, the context facing health care leaders across the countries of Europe is increasingly similar. Comparisons show that unlike in the private sector, where there is a financial bottom line, public services such as health care have an ambiguous accountability with a multitude of internal and external constituencies such as professional health care staff, politicians and patients' rights groups. One complication for the health sector, and public services generally, is that when facing a risk-taking decision, such as a large investment, the organisation must first think through the desired outputs before the means of measuring performance and results can be determined. This is because measuring the performance and impact of investments in health and health care services can be difficult. This public sector context has no parallel history in the private sector although in recent years considerable and frequently successful shareholder pressure has been felt by a number of commercial organisations worldwide. Despite these differences, what is common to both the public and private sectors across Europe is that it is in the decision that everything comes together. Managers across both sectors either make decisions effectively or they render themselves ineffective by making poor-quality decisions. However, research shows that decision-making is actually quite rare. Senior managers, whether in the public or private sector, actually spend far more time in meetings with people or in trying to get information (Kotter 1982). This reflects the leadership literature with its emphasis on influencing other people by building relationships and networks.

It is disappointing that the management science literature has few relevant studies focusing on leadership as a process. There are however three studies that are helpful in understanding how public service leaders work. Kotter and Lawrence (1974), in their study of US urban governance, identified five types of mayoral behaviour that occurred in three different but interrelated processes. The first process is deciding what to do; this means agenda setting, network building and task accomplishment. The second process is context, meaning the mayor's personality, the formal structure of city government and the distribution of power in the community and city. The final part of the process is the amount of authority given to the mayor by city government, which in turn influences the emergence of managerial behaviours by the mayor's office such as executive-type or entrepreneurial actions. In the UK, Leadbeater and Goss's (1998) five case studies of civic entrepreneurship in the public services highlight three ingredients that differentiate it from other kinds. First, it is as much about political renewal as it is about managerial change, meaning public organisations renewing their sense of purpose, which is largely a political process. Second, from a leadership perspective civic entrepreneurship is essentially about collaborative leadership, working across boundaries, and beyond organisations. Third, it is more than individual acts of innovation; it is about creating new services and products and exploiting the maximum social value from them.

Goodwin's research (2002) on chief executive leadership in the UK NHS draws two significant conclusions. First, it is the successful management of big local issues such as service and financial strategies that for chief executives and their teams creates a local leadership culture, which then forms a basis for further, successful implementation of major change. The extent to which a leadership culture can be successfully created is determined by the chief executive's ability to manage and explain the interaction between national and local objectives; and the extent to which the chief executive is influenced by, or personally influences the following variables:

- the quality of his or her executive team as perceived by external players;
- the impact of local relationships and local leaders;
- the creation of interpersonal and inter-organisational networks;
- the extent to which networks are used to create inter-organisational power sharing, alliances and partnerships.

Here is a practical example from the research. The chief executive of a UK health authority made a decision to close a local general hospital in order to reduce costs, with services being redistributed to other hospitals in the area. In taking the decision, the chief executive alienated local general practitioners (namely primary care physicians) because although they recognised the need to close a hospital, the one chosen for closure would not have been their first choice. The chief executive recognised that he had to re-establish working relationships with local general practitioners in the light of the closure decision. In order to do that, the chief executive created a new post of director of primary care, which would be filled by a general practitioner. This was successfully implemented and, over time, relationships with local general practitioners were re-established by the new director acting as an intermediary between the health authority and his general practitioner colleagues. This research is discussed more fully in Chapter 6.

NETWORKS AND NETWORKING

The above studies reflect the process-based approach to successful leadership, specifically: the creation of extensive networks, the value placed on interpersonal relationships, the clarity of the agenda for change, the importance of teams and the building of personal leadership credibility. The European context of health care leadership, with its emphasis on an inter-organisational and systems-based approach, makes networks and networking important to health care leadership success. Meurs (1997) has identified boundary crossing and creating interdependencies as important skills for health service managers in Europe; and crossing boundaries is essential since health care cannot be organised nor controlled from one centre. Successful management of health care organisations is reliant on bringing together different areas of knowledge, a process that should be facilitated by organisational leaders. Practical studies of how general managers work have also shown that they will often call on their entire network of work-based relationships to help implement their agendas. These managers will use tactics such as simply asking or suggesting that people take action, using resources to negotiate, exerting indirect influence through intermediaries, and occasionally using intimidation and coercion (Kotter 1999).

The *N-form* organisation

Networks by definition connect everyone to everyone else. Hierarchical organisations by definition do not do that and instead create formal channels of communication that everyone is expected to follow, although it has long been known that informal relationships in work are important. These networks of relationships account for regularities in day-to-day work; distinguish effective from ineffective individuals and groups; and generally provide key channels for getting things done. Research has confirmed what organisational leaders and managers intuitively already know, namely that patterns of informal network interactions play an important role in facilitating the achievement of individual and organisational objectives, but what is less known is the specific kinds of network patterns that lead to particular action outcomes (Ibarra 1992).

At least three types of interdependence between organisations have been identified: vertical, horizontal and symbiotic (Pennings 1981). Each form is the basis for a distinct type of exchange, with particular implications for the sustainability of collaboration. Vertical interdependence is a characteristic between organisations at different stages in the process of production. For example, the purchaser and provider roles arising from market-based approaches to the organisation and management of health care created new vertical interdependencies. Horizontal interdependence draws together functionally similar organisations around limited common interest, for example trade federations and associations or health care organisations and socio-economic development agencies. Symbiotic interdependence is comparable to productive exchange or incorporation in which if one person or organisation fails to perform properly, then neither or none will benefit.

Management research has documented the emergence of the network organisation as a distinct structural form that is neither market nor hierarchy: the so-called *N-form* organisation. But what are network and networking, and does network refer to certain characteristics of any organisation or to a particular form of organisation? Typically, the term network is used to describe the observed pattern of organisation but just as often it is used to advocate what organisations must become if they are to be successful (Nohria 1992). Some would argue that all known network organisations evolved unplanned or resulted from the re-design of a non-network organisation rather than be created as *N-form* from the beginning (Baker 1992). The chief structural characteristic of the *N-form* organisation is the high degree of integration across formal boundaries of multiple types of socially important relationships, for example task-related communication, informal socialising, advice giving and receiving, promotion decisions and so on. In a network organisation integration covers vertical (hierarchical) levels and spatial differentiation (multiple geographic locations) as well as horizontal differentiation.

The *N-form* organisation is characterised by lateral or horizontal patterns of exchange, interdependent flows of resources and reciprocal lines of communication (Ibarra ibid.). Importantly, a political perspective emphasises the importance of power and influence, and the factors that are seen to empower individuals in their network are: the contacts they have; their reputation, knowledge and expertise; their formal position and place in the status hierarchy of their organisation; and their alliances and group memberships. Others express that more simply, saying that personal credibility stems from two sources: expertise and relationships (Conger 1998). Within the integrative-based network system, power stems primarily from controlling information and influence is derived from expertise. In contrast, the most valued commodity in hierarchical systems is authority or standing within the hierarchy. While alliances are important in both types of system, personal characteristics define their usefulness to a greater extent in the network system than do task-relevant skills in hierarchies.

Types of network, power and personal attributes

The understanding of networks is limited because very little is known about how network patterns form, how stable they are or what is needed to change them. This is partly because networks are as much process as they are structure. They are being continually shaped and reshaped by the actions of individuals who are themselves constrained by the structural positions in which they find themselves both within the network and in their organisation. Consequently, more research is needed to determine the interrelationships between personal characteristics, strategies and tactics, and networks. Notwithstanding that, three different types of network have been identified (Brass and Burkhardt 1992): the workflow network, the communication network, and the friendship network, all terms that are self-explanatory. An organisation's environment can be viewed as a network of other organisations within which the environment consists of a field of relationships that bind organisations together. For leaders, networks not only set the context for the actions they wish to take, thereby providing resources and constraints, but they are also there to be manipulated in order to provide more resources and fewer constraints. This applies equally both inside and outside the organisation, health system or clinical service. The principles of managing networks are the same whether they are within or outside the organisation.

So how do networks operate? Within networks, levels of assertiveness and coalition building and power are correlated with individual position in the network relative to its centre and behavioural strategies such as influence, contacts and connections (Bass 1990; Brass and Burkhardt 1992; Kotter 1982; Yukl 1994). It follows that an individual who establishes links with other powerful people will increase their power. Caution is urged however since links may not increase individual power in certain situations; for example, while other powerful people may provide useful information in a communications network, negotiating with other powerful people in a bargaining network may produce negative results. What is important to know is that those who occupy central positions in a network that enable them to exercise control over the flow of information are most likely to emerge as leaders. In networks based on authority and in those based on information, the information typically flows in opposite directions. That is, information in networks based on authority flows down the hierarchy from those in positions of authority. In contrast, in information-based networks, the information primarily flows upward from those who provide information to those who collect it for use in decision-making. Therefore, there is potential for conflict particularly in hierarchical, strongly professionally based organisations such as in the health care sector because information tends to flow upwards and authority downwards.

It will come as no surprise to practising health care leaders that networks are an important source of soft data. Research shows that 'soft' information plays a valuable role in the performance assessment of health care organisations and is often used to complement the use of 'hard' information (Goddard *et al.* 1999). A simplistic distinction is that soft data is subjective and qualitative, while hard data is objective and quantitative. This generates the tendency to view hard data as being more valid or reliable than soft data, which can be seen as subject to bias and distortion. There is evidence that soft information is used to assess the quality of hospital services (Mannion and Goddard 2004). A study of UK general practitioners' assessments of hospital services showed that they are heavily influenced by informal sources of information, including the perceived reputation of individual hospital clinicians, the experiences of patients and the views of colleagues. Hard performance data about health care organisations can take up to a year to be published because of the time taken for the data to be collected, analysed and reported, for example in hospital annual reports and national league tables of hospital performance. The use of soft information is therefore timely and the authors urge caution in ensuring that valuable flows of soft information are neither suppressed nor distorted but instead, are used to complement hard performance data.

A key conclusion from the research of Goddard *et al.* (ibid.) is that hard information, when used in isolation is seen as inadequate and sometimes misleading to the performance of health care organisations. Trust is a key factor in the use of soft information to assess performance; for example, well-performing health care organisations are those in which the chief executive can be trusted to deliver agreed action rather than having to be chased up all the time. A further assessment of performance is the quality of the relationships between clinical staff and managers. Although there is a growing amount of hard data to assess clinical processes and outcomes, there is equal concern about the nature of the internal relationships within health care organisations.

Consequently, successful health care organisations are those that actively involve clinical staff in medico-managerial decision-making in the overall management of the organisation. There are of course drawbacks with placing too much emphasis on the use of soft information. There is the potential for obtaining biased or distorted views, largely because much soft information is collected in discussion with individuals who may be pursuing their own agenda. While formal indicators and hard data are used to assess the performance of health care organisations, they are usually supplemented with soft data in order to avoid forming an inadequate or misleading view. As the aforementioned comments about general practitioners (Mannion and Goddard ibid.) indicate, judgements will often be made in relation to the performance of health care organisations – and by implication their leaders – based on soft information drawn from a variety of informal sources and networks. The increasing use of soft information means placing a much greater emphasis on interpersonal- and network-based styles of management in order to obtain such information. This has implications for leaders in terms of time and personal skills development.

Unfortunately, network studies in the health sector are hard to find but two studies are useful in exploring the implications of developing network-based organisations for health and health care. In their study of UK health authorities Ferlie and Pettigrew (1996) identified the following key networking attributes and skills as important to success: strong interpersonal communications and listening skills, an ability to persuade, and an ability to construct long-term relationships. And in their policy report exploring key lessons for health care from networks across three other major industries, Goodwin *et al.* (2003) identify a number of challenges for the development of networks in health care. First, in a reflection of the literature, the first challenge for managers of networks is to understand the scope to which they are able to change their own position within it to secure or retain a central position from which to exert influence. This is important because from that position the manager has more ability to access resources from others in the network and provide a base from which to manipulate and/or steer the objectives of the network. Leaders matter in networks because they are necessary to promote the network to their peers. In health networks it was found that the leaders ideally should come from a professional or clinical background with a level of charisma. This reflects the findings that professionals within broader networks are distinct groups that respond best to charismatic leadership from one of their own.

Labianca *et al.* (1998) remind us that few network studies have considered negative affective or emotional relationships and their impact on inter-group conflict. They raise the interrelated questions of whether interpersonal relationships are the primary cause of inter-group perceptions or whether inter-group perceptions are the primary cause of interpersonal relationships. Importantly, they say that only laboratory-based experimental research can determine whether perceptions of inter-group conflict have a greater effect on interpersonal interactions or vice versa. Using social network analysis Labianca *et al.* (ibid.) conducted a small-scale, questionnaire-based study concluding, among other things that:

- negative as well as positive affect results from contact with others;
- numerous negative relationships within a group are associated with high perceived inter-group conflict with a focus on the latter often being used as an excuse by a group for not dealing with the former;
- individuals directly engaged in negative relationships with members of other groups perceived their entire own group as having a higher level of inter-group conflict.

The results underscore that negative information about others is weighted more heavily than positive or neutral information, which reflects the neuroscience aspects of emotional intelligence discussed in Chapter 5. It cannot be assumed that all members of a group are homogenous in their perceptions of inter-group conflict or that they have similar or no interpersonal relationships with members of other groups.

In working with networks, it is important to note that size of network is generally not an issue because the fundamental, interpersonal dynamics are always at work irrespective of the network's size (Wheatley 1999). In addition, leadership of networks is not necessarily dependent upon status; and consequently, network managers are important leaders whose skills and roles need development, support and nurturing by senior staff in the organisations supporting the network. But are there barriers to establishing relationships in networks? Baker (1992) statistically tested the extent to which formal organisational dimensions (namely formal position, geographical location or market group) are barriers to interpersonal ties. He identified that the chief executive officer (CEO) occupies a central cultural and structural position in the organisation, which in the analysis of strong ties, includes the CEO being surrounded by their senior team. However, the CEO is not a critical node in the negotiating networks. Although the CEO occupies a very central position, especially in strong-tie networks, removal of the CEO does not cause existing strong-tie and weak-tie networks to become substantially more or less integrated than they already are. This can be partly explained by a study of managers in three diverse US organisations, two of which are in the public sector (Luthans *et al.*

1985). It was found that for the more successful managers, networking with outsiders including socialising and politicking, has a statistically significant relationship to personal managerial success. However, top-level managers did not exhibit as much social and political networking although they did exhibit considerably more decision-making, planning and coordinating. It is clear that once a manager reaches the very top of an organisation or service, then they no longer need to depend upon social or political networking for reaching their personal career goal.

To network effectively both within and beyond organisations requires time, commitment and effort. The basis of good networking is the development of effective interpersonal relationships. When working within a network or when entering a network for the first time, the following simple guidelines, which apply equally to leaders at all levels of an organisation, may be helpful in establishing personal credibility, power and influence:

- Developing interpersonal relationships involves getting to know people, so when working across your organisation, service or network proactively speak to people instead of waiting for them to speak to you.
- Develop your personal credibility and power by listening to the views of others in the network and if possible, positively act on them.
- Similarly, ask people if they can help you or if you can help them.
- Establish your leadership, influence and power by putting people in touch with other people who can help them achieve their objectives.
- Leadership is concerned with people management so always maintain respect by showing gratitude for the work and effort of others.
- To enhance your interpersonal credibility learn people's names and keep in touch with them.

Although network-based working is increasing, generally out of business necessity and for the contextual reasons given in Chapter 3, networks are not a substitute for formal organisations. They are, however, a way in which complex agendas can be connected for delivery. Where there is complexity and uncertainty across a system, it is very unlikely that individual leaders acting alone at the top of organisations can be up to the challenge (Attwood *et al.* 2003). This means that they must learn to utilise and further develop the capabilities and capacities of their teams and other players and stakeholders in the system in which they are working. This requires self-knowledge and complementary capabilities of skills, knowledge and networks. It also requires humility and openness to respond positively to personal and professional challenges. This does not mean that there is never any disagreement or the airing of differences of view but players who operate in this way have developed the capability to act together as one. Dissent will and does occur but it is not ignored or put aside; rather, it is used to enrich understanding and develop creative ways forward.

MOVING FROM NETWORKING TO COLLABORATION

Whole system working

In their analysis of whole system working, Pratt *et al.* (1999) explore the theory of partnerships and distinguish between four different types of partnership behaviour: competition, cooperation, coordination, and co-evolution. Each type requires a different behavioural response to achieve its ends and when there is lack of clarity over the particular partnership type being pursued there is likely to be muddle and confusion, and frustration grows between the partners. The types of partnership are not organised in a hierarchy and nor are they discrete. Importantly, they may be dynamic because partnerships move between and across types over time. Their appropriateness and value depends on the goals being pursued and in particular, on whether these are collective or individual in character. There is also the issue of predictability, which may be high or low. In complex adaptive systems, of which health and social care are an example, it is often not possible to predict purpose or the requisite behaviour required in precise detail. Only broad aims may be recognised and achieving the required aims goal may depend on triggering changes in other partners that cannot be predetermined.

Competition can be a powerful stimulus for improving creativity and the efficiency of individual parts of a system. It is possibly the simplest form of partnership behaviour to achieve and the easiest to sustain as it requires no agreement between competitors and there are no uncertainties about what to do. In contrast, cooperation arises when the goal is individual but the partners see their future as linked. Cooperating partnerships do not need the time and effort required to reach a collective goal. What they require is a structure that penalises competitive behaviour and rewards cooperative behaviour. Cooperation may be encouraged if the desire is to:

- promote trust and long term sustainable relationships;
- create stability in relationships or avoid reorganisations or build expectations of length of stay in jobs;

- outlaw cost-shifting as having no place in a cooperative relationship;
- emphasise the benefits and strategies for cooperation through consistent and transparent decision rules.

The creation of joint posts between health and social care organisations are examples of cooperation.

Coordinating partnerships are linked with the intention of delivering predetermined, common objectives. The incentive may be a desire to reduce duplication, add value by pooling resources, or to fit the parts together more effectively. Coordinating partnerships are frequently limited to issues that do not challenge the objectives of the individual organisations involved. As such they rarely impinge on the core business of the partners who continue to pursue their own individual goals. They therefore rarely survive beyond a project period.

Finally, there is co-evolution. Partnerships are sometimes needed to generate new possibilities and new ways of working. The aim may be shared but less clearly defined than the predetermined objectives of coordination and there is no certainty of what works. In a co-evolving partnership behaviour occurs because the partners are committed to co-design something together for a shared purpose. It is not about past patterns or about coordinating good practice. Rather, it is about working into the future in ways that are not yet known. Partnership of this type is a vehicle for engaging with seemingly intractable problems and is intended as a 'whole systems' collective response. In the UK, the emergence of care trusts, in which health and social care services are integrated under common management, are examples of co-evolving partnerships.

Creating collaborative advantage

Although there is much talk of networking it is rarely explained in the context of systems and partnership working. The reality is that networking is a relatively simple and low-risk activity with little or no commitment required at the time it is undertaken. There is also the risk that networks absorb rather than unlock resources in the short and medium term, and become too preoccupied with discussion and process rather than with problem-solving and outputs. It is only when networking moves on to more formal working, often coupled with a commitment to reach joint agreements, that organisational and personal risk increases. Huxham (1996) coined the phrase *collaborative advantage* from work with large public sector organisations. It is concerned with the creation of synergy between collaborating organisations and their management teams. The definition of collaboration focuses on outputs that could not have been achieved except through collaborating. This is an important point because it is

Table 4.1 From networking to collaboration

Level	Category	Definition
1	Networking	The most informal level and therefore can be used most easily. Defined as exchanging information for mutual benefit. Involves little or no risk.
2	Coordination	This requires more organisational involvement than networking. Defined as exchanging information and altering activities for mutual benefit and to achieve a common purpose.
3	Cooperation	This too requires even greater organisational commitments and may involve legal arrangements. Defined as exchanging information, altering activities and sharing resources for mutual benefit and to achieve a common purpose.
4	Collaboration	Defined as exchanging information, altering activities, sharing resources and enhancing the capacity of another for mutual benefit and to achieve a common purpose. To do this requires sharing risks, responsibilities, resources and rewards, all of which can increase the potential of collaboration beyond other ways of working together. Collaboration is a relationship in which each person or organisation wants to help their partners become better at what they do.

emphasising the need for each individual organisation to achieve its own objectives better than it could alone, which is not only an ideal but also a necessary requirement of successful collaboration. Collaboration implies a positive, purposeful relationship between organisations that retains autonomy, integrity, and distinct identity, and thus the potential to withdraw from the relationship (Cropper 1996). Consequently, networking is only one level of activity along a developmental continuum of inter-organisational working that starts with networking, followed by coordination and cooperation, and finally ending with collaboration (see Table 4.1). To pursue leadership across systems requires a twofold approach: first, a facilitative style because of the multi-organisational basis of systems; and second, a focus on team working with a commitment to understand each organisation's culture and to work in genuine partnership.

Collaboration and stakeholders

For collaboration to be successful, the leader must consider other stakeholders. Stakeholders may be followers of the leader but they also may be leaders in their own right, particularly if they are leaders of other organisations or external professional or patients' groups. External stakeholders are independent players within the environment who fundamentally affect the context within which the organisation must work and yet have no direct role within the organisation. Leaders of services within organisations must also take into account stakeholders within their own organisations in proposed change programmes. For example, the leader of a surgical service planning major change would probably need to consult with a wide range of internal stakeholders such as hospital management, anaesthetics, theatre management, surgical supplies, and high dependency and intensive care. External stakeholders are largely uncontrollable by the organisation and so need to be treated as part of possible strategic futures. In his review of four governmental policy collaboratives in the Netherlands, de Jong (1996) differentiates between reactive and interactive approaches to inter-organisational working. In the first, policy is proposed but the resultant discussions can often result in an attack on the policy and subsequent defence from the policy originator. In contrast, the interactive approach focuses on policy being prepared through an interactive group process guided by an expert facilitator. Overall, the interactive approach has many advantages, especially for consensus building. However, the biggest challenge was found to be the availability of enough well-trained and experienced facilitators.

Categorising stakeholders helps to narrow a very large number of people and other organisations down to those that have the power to support or ruin the intent of the strategy-making organization or service. There are a number of obstacles to achieving successful collaboration that need to be taken into account when undertaking stakeholder analysis (Sink 1996). They include dealing with individual stakeholder idiosyncrasies, egos, personal agendas and interpersonal quirkiness, which is not surprising since it is people who make up collaboratives. The ability of people to get along and communicate strongly affects the outcomes of collaborative working. Leaders and facilitators (if they are employed) will need to be aware of the ways that personalities can affect group communications. Although hierarchies, networks, structures and strategy are all important in organisational and inter-organisational life, business is actually conducted by people sitting down with other people. Finally, it is important to note that although those public sector networks that are developed inclusive of all agencies and which identify improvements to user services as the basis of their work may produce better outcomes, inclusiveness of participation is time and resource intensive, which means that networks may not be able to reduce costs or make savings.

Partnership working

Partnership is an over-used term that embraces a range of collaborative relationships. It is necessary to be clear about the nature and purpose of a partnership in order to determine whether or not it has succeeded in improving the delivery and outcome of care across professional and organisational boundaries as perceived by stakeholders including users and their carers. The UK Audit Commission (1998) describes partnership as a joint working arrangement where the partners:

- are otherwise independent bodies;
- agree to cooperate to achieve a common goal;
- create a new organisational structure or process to achieve this goal, separate from their own organisations;
- plan and implement a jointly agreed programme, often with joint staff or resources;
- share relevant information;
- pool risks and rewards.

Partnerships vary greatly in both size and scope and there is no common model for success. The Audit Commission has identified four main models:

1 Separate organisation
  The partners set up a distinct organisation with a separate legal identity from that of the individual partners; it is most suitable for larger partnerships with a medium- or long-term lifespan and for those that need to employ staff and oversee large programmes of activity.

2 Virtual organisation
  The partners give the partnership a separate identity but without creating a distinct legal identity; at a formal level, one partner employs any staff and manages resources.

3 Co-locating staff from partner organisations
  This is a less formal model where a group of staff from the partner organisations work together to a common agenda usually under a steering group; sometime resources will be pooled to support the partnership's work but any staff continue to be managed separately by the partner that employs them.

4   Steering group without dedicated staff resources
     This is the simplest and least formal model and consists simply of a steering
     group without either dedicated staff or budget so its outputs must be
     capable of being implemented through the partners' mainstream organisa-
     tion and business.

After extensive research into partnership and collaboration Huxam and
Vangen (2000) conclude that given the strength of the forces that act against
success it is best not to pursue partnership unless it is necessary or unless the
participants can see the potential for achieving significant collaborative advantage. Consequently, one challenge for those thinking about partnership is
knowing when not to use the collaborative approach and being able to assess
when doing so would really make a difference. Among other things, this means
being selective in responding to policy incentives if at all possible. It is not
uncommon for organisations to leap into responding to national policies or
initiatives without thinking through the implementation issues or outcomes.
Being able to judge whether there is a sufficiently close fit to current organisational or business objectives is an important leadership skill. This means making
a judgement not only about the importance of the substance of the policy but
also about how the proposed partnership itself will relate to existing ways of
working. It may also mean persuading others who might potentially be involved
that it would not be wise to go ahead. There is also a challenge to policy makers
in devising incentives that allow potential policy recipients the flexibility to
adapt the proposed initiative to local context and circumstances.

    If a decision to go ahead with partnership working is made then further
challenges result. Keeping activity moving even though nothing will be done
perfectly and knowing how and when to compromise are obviously key challenges. Finding a workable level at which to agree aims, getting started in
building trust, gaining mutual understanding and dealing with the effects of
changing membership are other challenges. In summary, if you are seriously
concerned to achieve success in partnership, be prepared to nurture because
all activities associated with partnership require sensitivity and attention to
detail. Nurturing a network of relationships requires constant attention and
effort, which means accepting that significant resources and personal energy
need to be devoted to the partnership. Unfortunately, although it is tempting
to search for prescriptive advice on how to meet these challenges, there are no
easy rules of best practice partly because the demands of partnership pull in
contradictory directions and partly because the sheer volume of activity that
needs to be attended to is greater than most available resources would allow

for. The conclusion therefore is that to make partnerships work requires a sophisticated approach; being clear about the key areas in which energy is required and to have some sense of the issues involved in tackling that area.

MANAGING UPWARDS

In thinking through the implementation of a proposed change programme, the leader will also need to manage upwards because the next tier or person up the line in the organisational hierarchy is likely to be important to a successful outcome. The term 'managing upwards' is generally used to mean the process of consciously working with the tier above to obtain the best for your boss, you and your service or organisation. Managing upwards is part of effective networking because studies suggest that effective leaders make time and effort to manage relationships not only with their staff but also their bosses (Gabarro and Kotter 2004). It is self-evident that failure to secure support from up the line for a major change will severely minimise the probability of success for both the change and the leader. Lack of success could rebound on the leader and severely undermine their leadership position, which could result in the leader's demise. But managing upwards is not just a required networking activity at the time of pursuing change. If a leader does not establish an ongoing and positive relationship with their boss or the board this increases the risk not only when corporate or political support is needed as part of a change process but also when additional resources are required at other times. Alternatively, if the organisation or service is downsizing, how will the leader ensure it is not their service or department that bears the brunt? The main aim of successful upward management is to achieve mutual trust and support, to achieve a symbi-otic relationship through which the leader and their boss further each other's professional and personal ambitions.

Failing to devote sufficient personal time and energy to managing upwards could have a number of consequences not only for the leader but also for the leader's followers and the change they are collectively trying to achieve. There could be many reasons why successfully managing upwards is difficult. Some leaders may be overly sensitive of the pecking order and feel that they do not have the right to an adult, equal relationship with those who are senior, perhaps in age as well as position. This deference may be interpreted as indicating that the leader is not worthy of an equal relationship. On the other hand, some leaders may value economy of effort in this area and deliberately avoid contact with senior people that might threaten the leader's views or position. This is of course easier if the leader's seniors are physically located outside the organisation, because avoiding contact is harder if everyone is located on the same site. However, although maintaining physical distance may be easy, maintaining minimal or distant communication is not sustainable. It would be difficult for a leader to pursue a major change without having some discussion or briefing with the tier above, whether for resource, political or general support purposes. For chief executives wishing to pursue major change or significant investment, the discussion or briefing is likely to involve the organisation's board of directors.

At the heart of managing upwards are effective and trusting interpersonal relationships, which in turn requires clear, mutual communication. In the context of managing upwards this is easier said than achieved because it requires the leader to understand how their boss operates in his or her own interpersonal relationships. As a minimum it is essential you understand your boss's objectives and pressures, including those from his or her own boss, and recognise the boss's strengths, weaknesses and blind spots (Gabarro and Kotter ibid.). It is helpful to observe closely how the boss relates to others at the leader's own level and below including how they prefer to communicate, such as via meetings, email or telephone calls. Alternatively, perhaps the boss has one-to-one meetings with people, perhaps not just at business or management meetings but informally over coffee or lunch? Are there some people with whom the boss seems to have a more effective working relationship than with the leader? If so, what are the characteristics of that relationship? When is the boss most approachable? How often does the boss meet with others? Are there things that other people in the organisation or department do that seem to be particularly valued by those above? For example, do they mirror the boss's behaviour? Or are they particularly adept at clear and succinct communication?

Considering the above questions will help you think through how best to secure optimum political and corporate managerial support from your boss and the tier above. The solution is getting to know the boss as a person and to remember that if you succeed in your job, then your boss will also look successful. However, the boss is only one-half of the relationship and you also need to reflect on how you may be viewed in the relationship. What are your strengths and weaknesses and do you have any personal characteristics that inhibit the development of a successful relationship with your boss? The issue of self-awareness, which is essential if we are to see ourselves as others may see us, is discussed more fully in Chapter 5 on emotional intelligence. In the meantime, taking sufficient time and effort to manage upwards can increase the probability of a successful business relationship with your boss by the establishment of an effective and honest interpersonal relationship based on mutual expectation and dependability.

TRUST

Why trust is important

Trust is one of the core elements of any relationship, whether professional or personal. Trust is important in the relationship between governments and their electorates, it is crucial between collaborating organisations and it is at the core of relationships between people working together in organisations. To create strong interpersonal relationships, as the basis of effective inter-organisational collaboration, requires trust as an absolute necessity. Developing real trust can be hard in personal relationships between people who have chosen to be together and have years to work on it. It can be harder still in the work setting where people have little or no say in selecting their professional colleagues and where time is short. Consider then how much more difficult it is to develop trust in very large organisations or between different organisations. There are limits to the trust between colleagues or between the leader and follower, since everyone retains the option to end the relationship. Developing trust is important because if people trust each other and their leaders then they will not only be able to work through the disagreements that arise from time to time within and between organisations, but they will also be prepared to take risks in pursuing mutually agreeable objectives. If there is little or no trust then people will turn from the work they have to do, to focus instead on rumour, politics and thinking about their next job move.

Trust is not an absolute, but is dynamic and contextual. For example, in their book, *Trust Matters*, Bibb and Kourdi (2004) refer to an international survey focusing on whether others can be trusted. Scandinavians were the most trusting with nearly 70 per cent saying that they could trust others; respondents in the USA, Britain and France were the least trusting with less than 30 per cent saying they trusted others. These differences could be for a variety of reasons relating to the values, norms, orientations and contextual variables within the cultures concerned. What is important in all cultures is that trust is gained through actions, not words: it is what people do that is more important than what they say. And three different dimensions of trust must be in place for leaders and their organisations to be maximally effective (Galford and Drapeau 2003). They are personal trust, organisational trust and strategic trust. Personal trust exists when, for example, a chief executive is trusted as an individual and as a leader. When this type of trust is in place, people believe that the chief executive is honest, will do what they say they will do, will treat people fairly, and will make an effort to look out for the well-being of their followers. Organisational trust exists not only when the chief executive is trusted but also when people trust the chief executive's organisation. They trust, for example, that the organisation's policies will be honestly and fairly administered and implemented as stated.

Strategic trust exists when people have trust in and support the organisation's mission, and in how the organisation will execute and deliver that mission. What this means for leaders proposing to collaborate either within or between organisations, is that there must be a substantial degree of personal trust between the leaders involved if they are going to work successfully together. They must believe that the other is honest; they will do what they say they are going to do; and that they will be fair in the way that they do things. However, even if there is a high degree of personal trust between the leaders involved, this could be undermined by a lack of inter-organisational trust. One leader may view another as being supported by a weak management team or may think the leader does not have the degree of internal organisational influence that they claim, for example over clinical or other professional staff. Finally, even if there is a high level of both personal and organisational trust, this could be undermined by a lack of strategic trust. So, if one leader has personal trust in another and believes that they will implement what they have agreed, the first leader still may be mistrustful because the second leader's service or organisation has a history of being overly competitive, self-seeking or predatory in nature.

To develop trust successfully requires personal consistency of message and action, clear communication and a willingness to tackle awkward issues. This is no different from developing trust in personal relationships. In the workplace though there is an additional important principle of trust, which is competence: *I can trust you if I believe you are good at what you do but I cannot trust you if I doubt your technical skill or expertise.* There is also a community element to trust in work. Whether or not organisations work with computers and email, organisations that network either internally or with other organisations will see informal groups of like-minded individuals emerging. When these communities of like-minded people coalesce around a common problem or challenge they become communities of practice. In turn, communities of practice support trust because they create and validate competence, a role that is performed by functions in hierarchical companies. For example, a hospital chief executive may not know which surgeon is best but the other surgeons do.

How mistrust develops

There are actions and behaviour that should be avoided if trust is not to erode into mistrust. Sometimes the problem of developing trust is a person;

sometimes it is the organisational or service culture; sometimes it is the leadership. In general, breakdown in trust can be grouped into the following categories (Galford and Drapeau 2003; Bibb and Kourdi 2004):

Hidden agendas and inconsistent messaging

Hidden agendas is where someone appears to be doing or saying something for one reason but is actually acting from another, self-serving motive. Hidden agendas spawn organisational politics. Working in an environment where people are suspicious or unsure of other's agendas results in the withholding of information, the spreading of inaccurate information and generally self-protective behaviour. Pursuing hidden agendas often results in the sending of inconsistent messages, which is one of the fastest moving destroyers of trust because inconsistent messaging can occur anywhere within an organisation; between organisations and stakeholders; and at any level. The antidotes to inconsistent messages are straightforward although not necessarily easy to implement. Leaders need to think through their priorities and before broadcasting them, rehearse them alone or with a trusted advisor to ensure they are coherent and honest. Leaders are expected to set challenging objectives and commitments but they should not be unrealistic.

Incongruence and inconsistent standards

Lack of congruence is people saying one thing and doing another. When this happens people are not trusted. For example, if staff believe that the organisation or leader has favourites, their trust will be eroded. It is tempting to allow the most talented or innovative staff to live by different rules in order to retain them but this often generates cynicism throughout the rest of the organisation. Staff will come to see that there is a lack of authenticity about the leader and to be authentic the leader needs to say what they really think and feel in the context of being true to their personal values and beliefs.

Misplaced benevolence

This focuses on problematic behaviour such as incompetence and individuals with a consistently negative attitude, or people who are volatile. Sometimes problematic staff can be transferred to more suitable jobs; sometimes they can be coached, trained or surrounded by people who will help them improve; sometimes however they must be tackled directly and let go by the organisation. These situations cannot be ignored but if they are not addressed then not only will everyone else see the problem very early on but they will also feel the effects and blame the leader.

False feedback

Being honest about staff shortcomings is difficult, particularly when discussions are face-to-face. However, honesty is absolutely essential.

Failure to trust others

Some situations are so painful or politically difficult that it is easy to pretend they do not exist, for example, if there has been a major service failure or if someone is fired and there is no discussion at the next staff meeting. Leaders should not ignore issues that everyone else is whispering about behind closed doors. Such issues need to be brought out into the open, discussed openly and questions answered directly and honestly whether from staff or others outside the immediate service or organisation if the individual was involved in inter-organisational collaboration.

Rumour and gossip

When an organisation is in the midst of a complex initiative, change or crisis there are ample opportunities for trust to breakdown because levels of risk and personal stress are high. In such situations it is often the handling of the issue by the leader rather than the issue itself that is important. Staff and potentially other organisational stakeholders know that something important is going on but if they do not know the full story they will over interpret any small piece of information. Rumours circulate and in most cases, they will be negative rather than positive. To minimise any risks of organisational and people fallout, leaders need to tackle these situations as quickly as possible with open, transparent and direct communication.

Consistent corporate underperformance

If an organisation regularly fails to meet the expectations set by its leader or board or stakeholders then trust erodes rapidly. The solution for the leader is to be realistic when setting expectations and communicate as much as possible to everybody about why these particular aims have been set and how they can be met. The principle here is that the more knowledge people have about what lies behind expectations, the more likely they are to continue to trust the leader and the organisation, even in difficult times. And it is during these times when the real test of how far trust has been developed is seen.

In considering how leaders and followers respond to the above scenarios what matters in the first instance is not simply how much people know but how they react to what they do not know. If there is a strong negative reaction to an untoward issue then trust has not developed very deeply. If the reaction is more equivocal then some trust may remain. Given the opportunity people tend to be forgiving of occasional mistakes and failure if they understand the reasons why (failure is discussed further in Chapter 7). When an individual acts in ways that compromise the development of trust people often think it is because the individual is deliberately trying to manipulate but this may not be so. It could be for other reasons such as personal feelings of inadequacy; a desire to be liked; a need to fit in and to be accepted by the immediate work group, organisation or leader; or potentially more dangerous, some individuals may have a strong drive to exercise power and control over other people.

CONCLUSION

This chapter has focused on the practical importance of leadership as a process with a strong emphasis on the development of interpersonally driven networks as the basis for inter-organisational collaboration and partnership. What is important is that working and delivering through networks is more challenging than working in hierarchical organisations because more personal and team effort is required to both develop and maintain the network. And working on a partnership basis should not be undertaken without adequate preparation and an acknowledgement that more time will be required for results to be achieved. The same applies for inter-service, inter-departmental and inter-directorate working within the same organisation.

Networking involves people conducting business with other people and consequently, the process can be challenging because of the personal time and effort required to achieve successful networking. The process can be particularly challenging for people who are naturally introverted because the thought of striking up conversations with strangers may be daunting. But like it or not networking is an essential approach for today's leader and basic networking skills can be practised in the familiar environment of the workplace. For example, start by getting out and about. Instead of remaining in the office and delivering messages by email, deliver some personally, perhaps offer to discuss a work issue over an informal lunch rather than using a formal meeting; and spot opportunities for social-based work events to make contact with people from other parts of the organisation or other organisations in the network. The more experienced networker can consider joining outside networks such as professional and business associations. When meeting a valuable contact, do not just exchange business cards but write down brief reminders of the conversation, including pertinent personal and professional facts so that they can be used as prompts in future discussions. Finally, maintaining contact is important so initial meetings could be followed up, possibly asking for advice or useful information from time to time, which shows that the other person's opinion is valued. Finally, to summarise the key learning points for leading through networks, many of which will also apply when managing upwards:

1   The development of long-term relationships creates the best foundation for sustainable success for both networks and managing upwards.

2   Spending time on personal contacts and the development of interpersonal relationships is crucial when establishing a network, to making it work, agreeing inter-organisational objectives and to developing interpersonal and inter-organisational trust.

3   Interpersonal and inter-organisational trust is a key ingredient to networking, managing upwards and developing effective and sustainable partnership and collaboration.

4   Try to understand the three main agendas of other key players in the network or your boss when managing upwards: organisational, political and personal.

5   Be flexible and acknowledge that some positions and views cannot be changed. If possible, take time to discover what possibly could be changed and how, and what is non-negotiable.

6   If possible, choose the team for working across the network carefully and take time to prepare them for the work, particularly ensuring that the team members have the necessary complementary skills and knowledge: ideally their own networks of influence; that they get on with each other; and crucially, that each has good interpersonal skills because as has already been said, networking is about people doing business with other people.

7   Working in collaboration or partnership with other organisations is more challenging and complex than pursuing objectives within the same organisation. To help minimise the complexity when working through networks, keep the messages as simple and compelling as possible with an emphasis on positive change and key priorities for action.

8   Luck and timing also play their part in working in partnership or collaborating with other people, services and organisations. There are likely to be moments of potentially greater influence, perhaps when other partners in the network are under greater pressure for change or to deliver inter-organisational objectives, so looking out for that opportunity is an important network leadership skill.

If one variable had to be identified above all others as being more important to success in working through networks, whether in the same organisation, in other organisations or in managing upwards then it is trust. For that reason it is worth summarising again key trust issues. Trust is not an easy concept to pin down but it is essentially something we judge in others from their actions rather than their words. Consequently, we develop the trustworthiness of others by interacting with them over time and specifically, from our perceptions of their ability, benevolence, integrity and honesty. It is not surprising therefore that people use their feelings as information when making judgements about others and so there are links with the concept of emotional intelligence that will be discussed in Chapter 5. Trust is hard to measure and even if it were quantifiable, no organisation or individual would ever be likely to achieve a perfect rating because organisations and people are too complex for such simple measurement. However, people generally know when trust exists but because it is an actions-based concept, it is difficult to hold it up to the light for examination. It can also be difficult to describe the trustworthy leader except in the context of actions, but it should be remembered that it is not possible to be a leader, or last long in a leadership role, without being trusted. Like leaders who are trusted, people who are trusted by others within and beyond the organisation come in different shapes and sizes: there is no correlation. What will link them all is that they are all human and consequentially, from time-to-time they will make an occasional mistake that may well erode some of their trust-based relationships. The strength of the underlying relationship between key individuals within the network will largely determine whether the mistake will adversely affect the working of the network. In summary, trust is a core component of organisational, inter-organisational and personal effectiveness and paying the necessary attention to developing it must be at the top of every leader's personal development plan.

DISCUSSION QUESTIONS

1   Are you aware of the networks that your service and organisation participates in and what the network objectives are as a result of that participation?
2   Consider the networks that you are familiar with in the context of the four levels in Table 4.1 above. Can you categorise each of the networks and differentiate between them from your own experience?
3   Are you in a position to lead or support moving the network up one or more levels in order to improve network effectiveness?
4   If you participate in networks are you clear about your role and what you have to achieve in terms of objectives?
5   Is there sufficient information and support to enable you to achieve your objectives?
6   If you are working with and/or supporting others in the network are you clear whether they have sufficient support to achieve their objectives?
7   Do you understand the value that trust plays in the work you do in your service, organisation or inter-organisational networking?
8   Are there aspects of the work that could be made more effective by the development of greater trust? If so, are there actions that you could take to help achieve that?

BIBLIOGRAPHY AND FURTHER READING

Attwood M., Pedlar M., Pritchard S. and Wilkinson D. (2003) *Leading Change. A guide to whole systems thinking.* Bristol: The Policy Press.

Audit Commission (1998) *A Fruitful Partnership: effective partnership working.* London: Audit Commission.

Baker W.E. (1992) The network organisation in theory and practice. In Nohria N. and Eccles R.G. (eds) *Networks and Organisations: structure, form and action.* Boston: Harvard Business School Press, pp. 397–429.

Bass B.M. (1990) *Bass and Stogdill's Handbook of Leadership Theory, Research and Managerial Applications.* New York: The Free Press.

Bibb S. and Kourdi J. (2004) *Trust Matters for Organisational and Personal Success.* Hampshire, UK: Palgrave Macmillan.

Brass D.J. and Burkhard M.E. (1992) Centrality and power in organisations. In Nohria N. and Eccles R.G. (eds) *Networks and Organisations: structure, form and action.* Boston: Harvard Business School Press, pp. 191–215.

Conger J.A. (1998) The necessary art of persuasion. *Harvard Business Review* May–June: 84–95.

Cropper S. (1996) Collaborative working and the issue of sustainability. In Huxham C. (ed.) *Creating Collaborative Advantage*. London: Sage, pp. 80–100.

De Jong A. (1996) Inter-organisational collaboration in the policy preparation process. In Huxham C. (ed.) *Creating Collaborative Advantage*. London: Sage, pp. 165–175.

Ferlie E. and Pettigrew A. (1996) Managing through networks: some issues and implications for the NHS. *Academy of Management Journal* 7: 81–99.

Gabarro J.J. and Kotter J.P. (2004) Managing your boss. *Harvard Business Review* Special Issue: 92–99.

Galford R. and Drapeau A.S. (2003) The enemies of trust. *Harvard Business Review* February: 89–95.

Goddard M., Mannion R. and Smith P.C. (1999) Assessing the performance of NHS Hospital Trusts: the role of 'hard' and 'soft' information. *Health Policy* 48: 119–134.

Goodwin N. (2002) *Determining the leadership role of chief executives in the English NHS*. Unpublished PhD thesis. Manchester Business School, University of Manchester.

Goodwin N., Perri 6, Peck E., Freeman T. and Posaner R. (2003) *Managing Across Diverse Networks of Care: lessons from other sectors*. Policy Report. Birmingham: Health Services Management Centre.

Huxham C. (ed.) (1996) *Creating Collaborative Advantage*. Sage: London.

Huxham C. and Vangen S. (2000) What makes partnerships work? In Osborne S. (ed.) *Public–Private Partnerships*. London and New York: Routledge.

Ibarra H. (1992) Structural alignments, individual strategies, and managerial action: elements toward a network theory of getting things done. In Nohria N. and Eccles R.G. (eds) *Networks and Organisations: structure, form and action*. Boston: Harvard Business School Press, pp. 165–188.

Kotter J.P. (1982) *The General Managers*. New York: The Free Press.

Kotter J.P. (1999) What efffective general managers really do. *Harvard Business Review*. Reprint 99208. March–April.

Kotter J.P. and Lawrence P.R. (1974) *Mayors in Action. Five approaches to urban governance*. New York: Wiley.

Labianca G., Brass D.J. and Gray B. (1998) Social networks and perceptions of intergroup conflict: the role of negative relationships and third parties. *Academy of Management Journal* 41(1): 55–67.

Leadbeater C. and Goss S. (1998) *Civic Entrepreneurship*. London: Demos.

Luthans F. , Rosenkrantz S.A. and Hennessey H.W. (1985) What do successful managers really do? An observational study of managerial activities. *The Journal of Applied Behavioural Science* 21: 255–270

Mannion R. and Goddard M. (2004) General practitioners' assessments of hospital quality and performance. *Clinical Governance: An International Journal* 9(1): 42–47.

Meurs P.L. (1997) *New Skills for the Health Care Manager.* Paper presented at the European Health Management Association Annual Conference. 27 June. The Netherlands.

Nohria N. (1992) Introduction: is a network perspective a useful way of studying organisations? Nohria N. and Eccles R.G. (eds) *Networks and Organisations: structure, form and action.* Boston: Harvard Business School Press, pp. 1–22.

Pennings J.M. (1981) Strategically interdependent organizations. In Nystrom P.C. and Starbuck W.H. (eds) *Handbook of Organizational Design. Vol. 1: Adapting Organisations to their Environments.* Oxford: Oxford University Press, pp. 433–455.

Pratt J., Gordon P. and Plamping D. (1999) *Working Whole Systems: putting theory into practice in organisations.* London: King's Fund.

Sink D. (1996) Five obstacles to community-based collaboration and some thoughts on overcoming them. In Huxham C. (ed.) *Creating Collaborative Advantage.* London: Sage, pp. 101–109.

Wheatley M.J. (1999) *Leadership and the New Science. Discovering order in a chaotic world.* San Francisco: Berrett-Koehler.

Yukl G. (1994) *Leadership in Organisations.* New Jersey: Prentice-Hall.

Chapter 5

Leadership and emotional intelligence

KEY POINTS OF THIS CHAPTER

- Leadership is as much about the 'how' as the 'what' and self-awareness is central to successful leadership.

- Effective leaders must possess a high degree of emotional intelligence, which means being concerned with the domains and competencies of personal and social skills.

- Emotional intelligence can be developed in most people and personal and social skills can be learned through a mixture of self-awareness, coaching, training and experience.

- Cultural intelligence – the ability to interpret unfamiliar and ambiguous gestures and behaviours from a local cultural perspective – is likely to become important with workforce movements across Europe.

- Leaders need to rely on the skills and experience of others in their team; and insisting on gender and ethnic diversity may be the only way to ensure a team considers a wide range of options and opinions.

- All-male leadership cultures should be avoided because women tend to have stronger empathy and relationship skills than men.

- Leaders need to recognise and manage their own anxiety. Being self-aware of your own emotions and the impact they have on others is as important as being aware of the emotions of others.

- There are links between emotional intelligence and intuition or gut feeling.

- Leaders occasionally need to show their human side by admitting mistakes and showing their weaknesses.

KEY TERMS

- Emotional intelligence or EQ
- Self-awareness
- Intuition and gut feeling
- Cultural intelligence
- Leadership teams
- Neo-cortex and limbic system
- Groupthink

INTRODUCTION

The last chapter emphasised that leadership is not just about what leaders do but equally importantly, how they do it. Ask people to talk about leadership and they will say that it is about inspiration, vision and creativity. It is all those things but it is also about challenge and focus on change. Consequently, leadership can be difficult, risky and occasionally painful. Also, leadership sometimes has little or no guarantee of success. Consider the task for the modern political and business leader and how potentially daunting and lonely leadership can be in an age of anxiety heralded by the continual fear of economic recession and terrorism. At such times it is essential for leaders to stay the course and learn how to sustain themselves in the eyes of their followers. The management guru Warren Bennis says that self-awareness is central to being a successful leader and he called the management of self – knowing your skills and deploying them effectively – a leadership commandment. Without it leaders and managers can do more harm than good. Like incompetent doctors, incompetent managers can make organisational life worse: making people sicker and feel less vital. This is why emotional intelligence is important. Leadership is an interpersonal dynamic process and consequently, leaders will fail if they cannot drive emotions in the right direction, whether their own or those of their followers. Leadership works through emotions and emotional intelligence is concerned with how leaders handle themselves and their relationships with others. Charisma is also linked to the idea of emotional intelligence, which in this context is concerned with abilities of persuasion and communication.

Goleman *et al.* (2002) argue that certain human competencies, such as self-awareness, self-discipline, persistence and empathy are of greater significance and importance than traditional intelligence, or IQ, in much of life. The concept of emotional intelligence focuses on being intelligent about emotions but it is important to understand that it is not about being emotional. Leaders need to be able to manage distressing emotions, whether in themselves or others, so they do not get in the way of their work. For example, when Rudolf Giuliani, the former Mayor of New York, was asked to speculate on the number of deaths caused by the terrorist attack on the World Trade Center in September 2001, he said that whatever the final count it would be more than any of us can bear. His response shows how compassion and displays of emotion can and should be allowed to surface in a difficult situation.

The executive of 50-years-ago may not have understood that effective leaders must possess a high degree of emotional intelligence, and that their success would depend on self-awareness, self-regulation, motivation, empathy and social skills. In today's world however, emotional intelligence could explain why the smartest person in the organisation has not progressed to the top or why someone who is outstandingly successful is not very bright. Emotional intelligence is about a different way of being smart and it has nothing to do with basic intelligence or IQ. When IQ scores are compared with career achievement, intelligence counts for only a quarter of the difference between high and low achievers (Goleman *et al.* ibid.). The rest is dependent on personal and social skills or emotional intelligence. Consequently, self-awareness – knowing yourself – is an essential part of becoming a leader and crucially, those without it will struggle to develop their emotional intelligence. It is important to remember that everything we do, say, hear and feel is influenced by how we see ourselves.

Developing sustainable, long-term success is the Holy Grail of leadership. To help achieve that necessitates us having to know ourselves even though achieving that can be very difficult. Until leaders know themselves, their strengths, weaknesses, the impact their presence has on others, what they can do and why they want to do it, they cannot succeed in any but the most super-ficial sense of the word. The better that leaders know themselves, the better they can make sense of the often incomprehensible and conflicting messages they receive every day from their staff and their working environment. This is not about searching for perfection because as a leader or as a person perfection is neither natural nor particularly human. What it is concerned with, however, is pursuing personal development in order to continue growing through our working and personal lives.

In summary, good leadership demands more than putting on a good face every day. It requires a leader to determine, through personal reflection, how emotional leadership drives the moods and actions of the organisation and then with equal discipline to adapt personal behaviour accordingly. Emotions can be useful to the development of a service and organisation. Aggression can be focused onto being the best; passion will drive the visionary leader; and for the service-based health care organisation how can it understand the consumer perspective without emotion? Leaders fail if they cannot drive emotions in the right direction and nothing will work as well as it could or should. This is why emotional intelligence is crucial to leadership success.

WHAT IS EMOTIONAL INTELLIGENCE?

Background

Emotional intelligence or EQ as it is known, is based on the concept of the ability of leaders and managers to understand and manage their emotions and relationships and this is the key to better personal, team and group performance (Goleman *et al.* ibid.). Scientifically, EQ is a synthesis of psychology, neurobiology and anthropology that shows how a leader's mood can energise or deflate an organisation. There is a relationship between the emotional centres of the brain, which pump out emotions and the neo-cortex, pre-frontal brain, which needs to take in information, understand it clearly and respond flexibly. Practically, emotional intelligence encompasses a set of day-to-day skills, most of which can be learned. One definition of EQ is the ability to recognise the meanings of emotions and their relationships and to reason and problem-solve on the basis of them. Emotional intelligence is involved in the capacity to perceive emotions, assimilate emotion-related feelings, understand the information of those emotions and manage them. If you are not convinced about the importance of emotional intelligence then start by asking if you are concerned about any of the following in your work:

- your influencing skills, because you want to understand others around you more in terms of what persuades them, what they actively listen to and really hear to be influenced;
- the performance of your immediate team and how to improve it, particularly when faced with difficult or potentially stressful organisational or inter-organisational challenges;
- stressful situations that get on top of you and cause you to be anxious about them hours after they have occurred or which wake you up in the night;
- getting the message across to people unambiguously and being able to listen without inner doubt disrupting your concentration;

- your work–life balance because you want it to become more equitable and less stressful;
- relationships that are stressful or events that are mystifying in terms of your own behaviour or the reactions of others;
- your general health because it is below par and you suspect it is self-inflicted in the form of bad work habits and a lack of commitment to good health.

If one or more of the above issues concerns you in how you undertake your leadership role, implement your objectives or establish your interpersonal and inter-organisational relationships, then emotional intelligence is very relevant. The reason is because people who have high emotional intelligence find it easy to empathise with other people and to use this to generate better results from a situation. People who have the ability to empathise will be better placed to push forward policies for change in their organisations or services. In short, people with high emotional intelligence tend to make better leaders than those with low emotional intelligence. Essentially, being a good leader requires the same qualities it takes to be a good human being. There are four components to emotional intelligence:

1 personal- or self-awareness, which is concerned with understanding your emotions, strengths and vulnerabilities;
2 conscious filters or self-management, which focuses on managing your personal motives and regulating behaviour;
3 context or social awareness is concerned with understanding what others are saying and feeling and why;
4 relational skills or relationship management meaning acting in such a way that you are able to get desired results from others and reach personal goals.

Emotional intelligence is concerned with both personal and social skills. Consequently, personal understanding of the above domains of emotional intelligence and their associated competencies is crucial to leadership success. The personal competencies are all about the individual: self-awareness, self-regulation and motivation; the ability to understand personal emotions and how they affect others; knowing strengths and limitations but having a self-confidence to commit and achieve; the ability to take the initiative and to be optimistic about the outcome; and the ability to cope with new things. It is our personal social skills that determine how people relate to others: the ability to sense other people's feelings and read the mood of a group; to inspire and build relationships; to work in teams; to listen and communicate. These skills can make a difference between success or failure in leadership. There are obvious links with trust that were discussed in the last chapter. To recap, trust is the expectancy of people that they can rely on the leader's word. It is built through the leader's consistency and integrity in relationships, which can be developed by sharing information, showing a willingness to be influenced, avoiding abuse of team members, being fair and delivering what the leader says they will deliver. In summary, trust focuses on telling the truth, being honest, treating everyone fairly and delivering agreed objectives.

The neuroscience of EQ

There are links between emotional intelligence and intuition or gut feeling. It is not particularly surprising to experienced executives to know that many people rely on their intuition to solve complex problems when logical methods, such as quantitative analysis, do not provide all the answers, particularly when trying to determine the reaction of others to possible strategic futures or solutions to complex issues (Hayashi 2001). The reality is that the further people progress in their careers the more likely they will need well-honed business and decision-making instincts. Every contact point with life creates a gut feeling, sometimes this is described as 'butterflies in the stomach' or a 'knot of intestinal tension or excitement'. Whether or not we acknowledge our 'gut reactions' they are shaping everything that we do just as they shape everything that everyone around you does, all the time. But what is intuition and gut feeling? The brain is intricately linked to other parts of the body through an extensive nervous system as well as through chemical signals such as hormones and neurotransmitters. Consequently, some neuroscientists assert that the mind is really an intertwined system comprising the brain with the body and that we actually have three brains (Cooper 2000). In addition to the head, we have brains in the gut and in the heart. The highest reasoning involves all three brains working together; it means we can ask better questions sooner and make better, clearer choices and decisions.

It is worth explaining the basic science of the concept of the three brains (Cooper ibid.; Goleman 1998; Goleman et al. 2002). The brain in the gut is known as the enteric nervous system and it is independent of but interconnected with the brain. There are more neurons in the intestinal tract than in the entire spinal column and this complex circuitry enables the enteric nervous system to act independently, learn, remember and influence our perceptions and behaviours. After each experience has been digested by the enteric nervous system, it is the heart's turn to ponder it. In the 1990s scientists in the emerging field of neurocardiology discovered that just as the brain in the gut uses its neural circuitry to act independently, learn, remember and respond to life, so does the brain in the heart. It is interesting to note that one of the heart's messenger chemicals is atrial peptide, which is a primary driver of motivated behaviour (Cooper ibid.). The third stop for nerve impulses is an area at the base of the brain known as the medulla. This is a vital link to the recticular activating system or RAS which connects with major nerves in the spinal column and brain. The RAS acts as filter of the one-hundred-million impulses the brain receives each second, deflecting the trivial and letting the vital through to alert the mind.

The RAS has evolved over millions of years and although the world has changed dramatically in that time, we still face everyday life with deeply embedded traits of our Stone Age ancestors. Their preoccupation for day-to-day survival was much greater than ours is today and there was a greater interest in negative messages being amplified. This explains why we can become anxious and defensive when someone expresses a few well-intended words of criticism while a genuine compliment is not given the same weight by the RAS. So, when we have had a good day with many things going well and perhaps only one thing going slightly wrong, nearly all of us become preoccupied with the one thing that went wrong. Consequently, if we do not learn to manage the RAS's negative influence, it can dominate our approach to life and stifle personal progress. After the RAS, neural communications travel to the limbic system, otherwise known as the emotional centre of the brain. It also functions up to eighty-thousand times faster than the thinking brain's cerebral cortex. Because the limbic system governs feelings, impulses and drives it is where we perceive the world and shape our response to it.

Why is this summary of the neuroscience important to our personal and leadership development and how does the science operate in practice? It is because prior to neurological based impressions reaching the thinking area of the brain, each experience has been sensed and interpreted by the gut, heart and other brain regions. In other words, we think last and not first. Consequently whenever we over-rely on the brain and the head, needless extra struggles appear because we can take decisions and leadership actions that may be analytically correct but they do not feel right. One reason is that whenever it operates without being balanced by the gut and heart, the intellect exists primarily as an act of convenience. It can conjure up all kinds of theories, principles and beliefs but even if these are well intentioned, they are not significant by themselves. This is because we have to feel things in order to live them. Of course we must think as clearly and insightfully as possible but without the active involvement of what we feel in our heart and gut the brain will become paralysed with objective analysis.

How does the science operate in practice? Imagine that you are walking alone in a remote area and suddenly come across a large ferocious animal. What happens right before you are consciously aware of the danger? As the above description of the science indicates, the image of the animal quickly passes from our eyes to the brain where the information reaches the visual thalamus, which is then related to the amygdala. A component of the limbic system that plays a key role in emotional emergencies, the amygdala begins sending instructions to the body. When survival is at risk, the body pumps in adrenaline to prepare for fight or flight. Sugars, cholesterol and fatty acids are released into the blood stream and blood pressure and heartbeat increases. Primed for action, the body reacts with either the fight reactions of anger, aggression and hostility or the flight emotions of terror, anxiety and nervousness. The adrenaline surge in the body gives the best chance for short-term survival, a natural reaction to fear that triggers an energy level used to increase awareness and optimise performance. If people freeze when confronted with danger then it is because the necessary adrenaline is lacking. This is the emotion of fear, which is the strongest and most powerful primal emotion. In today's alternative, modern-day scenario of the gut instinct telling an organisational leader to change decisions or promote one person over another, the feelings are obviously much more subtle and complex but they are still present. But there is an important link between the two scenarios. First, the mind continuously processes informa-tion that we are not consciously aware of, not only when we are asleep and dreaming but also when we are awake. This helps explain the 'of course' reac-tion when we learn something that we actually already knew. In other words, the sense of revelation at the obvious occurs when the conscious mind finally learns what the subconscious mind had already known.

EQ and personal leadership development

Managing work life is not always easy and for many it can be a difficult chal-lenge. Accurately gauging how emotions affect others can be just as difficult. Although most leaders care how others perceive them very often they incor-rectly assume that they can interpret this for themselves. However, in general, leaders do not really know if they have resonance with their organisations. The research of Goleman *et al.* (2001) identified 'CEO disease' with its single symptom of near-total ignorance by the CEO about how his or her mood and actions appear to the organisation. Although leaders think that if they are having a negative effect someone will tell them, they are wrong. This explains why many chief executives will say that they often feel they are not getting the truth from people in their organisation. This does not mean people are lying to them but the reality is that information is being hidden or massaged. The fact is that people do not tell leaders the whole truth about the impact their emotions are having on others for many reasons. Sometimes people are frightened of being the bearer of bad news and consequentially suffering personally and professionally. Other people will feel that it is not their place to tell their boss the truth about an organisational issue, while others do not realise that what they really want to talk about is the very effect of the leader's emotional style. Consequently, leaders cannot rely on their followers to spontaneously present the full picture.

To develop and apply an exceptional level of emotional intelligence in life and work, we must combine the perceptions and impressions of the human gut, heart and mind. If we operate with old mind-sets, assuming that the old facts about human motivation and work relationships are still correct, we are wasting large amounts of energy, time and money – and falling far short of the results we could achieve. This then helps explain why uncertainty, fear or intuitive feelings are frequently accompanied by physical reactions such as a faster heartbeat or the feeling of 'butterflies' in the stomach. When we use our gut, we are drawing on rules and patterns that we cannot quite articulate. We are reaching conclusions on the basis of things that go on in our perceptual system where we are aware of the result of the perception but we are not aware of the steps. It is to distinguish between the two kinds of thought that the terms 'left brain' for the conscious, rational and logical, and 'right brain' for the subconscious, intuitive and emotional have been formed. Many executives have learned to tap into their right-brain thinking by jogging, daydreaming, listening to music or using other relaxation techniques. Finding time for right-brain development should be a key personal development activity.

Above all else, we need to keep tapping into all of our sources of wisdom and insight, not just one. Each time we face an important moment during the day, we need to ask ourselves what does my gut say about this? My heart? My head? We need to listen clearly to each of these three streams of intelligence as we decide how to act or interact. Second, we need to make sure our words are consistent with what we feel inside. Remember that others can often sense how we feel, whether in person or listening on the telephone. When people hear something that seems to be at odds with what the speaker is really feeling, nearly everyone instantly bets on the feelings, not the words. So, when you say things are 'fine, don't worry, I have it all under control', there are two likely reactions by others. The first is that you are seen as being dishonest because the hearts and guts of your staff and followers can sense that you do not have everything under control. The second reaction is that they tend to assume things may be even worse than they actually are and more importantly, they will impart this view to others. Rumour and gossip become amplified and spread very quickly. Consequently, any trust that you have developed with staff and stakeholders dissipates quickly.

The optimum approach is to recognise others for each effort, genuinely, specifically and individually because performance is high when people are given frequent, sincere encouragement. Many of us have come to tolerate the absence of respect and to expect poor recognition or none at all, every time we make an effort or contribution. Without it however, no one will give their best or at least not for long. Before giving recognition consider personalising your comments to the person you are speaking to. Individualise your remarks for members of a group and try and thank more than one person, singling out each individual if possible. Most people tend to praise a whole group, yet no matter how sincere they may be, they inadvertently make every one of these individuals feel devalued and invisible. Before thanking a group, learn at least one specific contribution that each individual has made to the success of the project for the service, network or organisation. Then when you thank the team you can mention something specific about the contribution of each individual.

However, instinct is not always right. Care is needed because instincts can often be wrong as various traits of human nature can easily cloud decision-making. For example, some people will often take unnecessary risks to recover a loss or correct a process that is going wrong. Another potential pitfall is a tendency to see patterns where none exist, what statisticians call 'over-fitting the data'. Or people may pursue a self-fulfilling prophecy, for example promoting someone and consciously or subconsciously making extra efforts to ensure that person's success. In the end the decision is justified but the process to secure success obscures whether the decision was a good one.

Another factor to take into account is that people have a tendency towards over-confidence. They tend to over-estimate their ability in just about everything such as driving, physical endurance and the ability to assess whether other people are telling the truth or not. In summary, people are a lot less capable than they think and most probably have only a 50:50 chance of detecting lies. To avoid such pitfalls, good leaders need to possess a powerful self-checking mechanism. Generally, this involves reflective time to review decisions they have made, and to identify learning from those decisions that will help when confronted with similar situations in the future, particularly if the decisions resulted in failure. Ideally, such self-assessment should be continual throughout a decision-making process; time should be found to stop to review progress. Good questions for leaders to ask are: why are we continuing to do this: do we have the right strategy and tactics; is what we are doing right for the service or organisation or network; are we making this decision for the right reasons; do we have support from all the right people with what we are trying to do and if not why not?

ASSESSING AND MANAGING EMOTIONAL INTELLIGENCE

Assessing EQ

There are various tools and questionnaires that are readily available to assess emotional intelligence but what do the results of an average test look like and how can they be used for personal development? To illustrate that, some years ago the author undertook such an assessment to help develop his own emotional intelligence and the report, which was produced following analysis of a self-completed questionnaire, looked like this:

> The level of emotional intelligence is within the average range, meaning that a degree of awareness and understanding of personal feelings exists but the ability to take account of these when making decisions can be somewhat variable. There would be times when feelings about specific issues would rise to the surface and swamp other thoughts resulting in occasional difficulty in achieving personal goals or desired outcomes in the face of your personal mood. . . . You are somewhat self-motivated and can take a long-term view of decisions. However, you may find that challenges and rejections of ideas and proposals tend to cause you to look for alternative strategies for realising goals without exploring the value of pursuing and re-framing your original ideas. You may find that facing the conflict associated with pursuing your plans is sufficiently uncomfortable to warrant your pursuing a less than ideal (in your view) strategy.

The report also made reference to the author's EQ and group working:

> In group situations . . . you recognise the importance of balancing soft and hard issues and considerations in making decisions. However, you tend to be more comfortable in focusing on objective and hard data in arriving at a decision. You will tend to find a degree of stress in your

working life and attempt to deal with this by attempting to impose a degree of control over the process of achieving results and making decisions. When working with a group you tend to be aware of the overall pulse of relationships but are not always comfortable in ensuring that feelings or emotions are brought to the surface. Whilst you may feel a need to take a leading role in a group you may hesitate to do so due to concerns over others' willingness to accept such a lead. . . . Whilst you recognise that conflict may be constructive in a group and needs to be surfaced, you feel uncomfortable in raising difficult issues and surfacing conflict.

In commenting on how to develop emotional intelligence, the report suggested that the author should follow the following action plan to build on the strengths of his existing emotional intelligence:

- reflect on and identify examples of behaviour you exhibit in different situations;
- focus on those behaviours that align with the strengths noted in this report and develop plans to reinforce and build on these;
- identify those behaviours that align with the development needs noted in this report and identify changes you could make to address these needs;
- consciously practice reinforcing and changing behaviours, and reflect on your responses to these;
- actively seek feedback from others on the impact of your changed behaviours.

The approach of this action plan is positive because unlike most training approaches for developing emotional intelligence and leadership skills it does not target the neo-cortex, the part of the brain that governs analytical and technical ability. Such approaches are most likely to fail. Instead, the action plan targets the limbic system, which controls feelings, impulses and desires. However, the limbic brain is a much slower learner particularly when the challenge is to re-learn deeply ingrained habits. Consider for example, how long it can sometimes take children to break bad or socially unacceptable habits. When the right model is used, training can actually alter the brain centres that regulate negative and positive emotions creating long-term improvements in EQ skills. The key is personal reflection and self-directed learning, which means intentionally developing or strengthening an aspect of who you are or who you want to be or both. The process involves five phases:

1   uncovering your ideal self, in other words who you want to be, how you want to behave and how you want to be seen by others;

2   determining your strengths and weaknesses;

3   creating a personal learning agenda for building on your strengths while filling in the gaps;

4   experimenting with and practising new behaviours, thoughts and feelings;

5   developing supportive and trusting relationships that make change possible by providing honest and confidential feedback.

Personal and social skills can be learned through a mixture of self-awareness, personal reflection, coaching, training and experience. Seeking direct feedback from trusted people at work or from a mentor or coach is one way of finding out whether you have personal and social skills. The workplace also provides lots of opportunity for practising other skills such as improving your contribution in meetings or improving presentational skills. Personal development, mentoring and coaching are covered in Chapter 7.

CULTURAL INTELLIGENCE

European Union policies on the free movement of labour and the facilitating of cross-border consumer choice of health care goods and services raises questions about the challenges of working and providing services in different cultures. Culture is very powerful and it is no surprise that human behaviour in a foreign country can be subject to an even wider range of interpretations, which may make misunderstandings likely and cooperation limited or impossible. But there are exceptions and occasionally an outsider has a seemingly natural ability to interpret someone's unfamiliar and ambiguous gestures in the same way that person's colleagues would. This is called cultural intelligence or CQ (Earley and Mosakowski 2004). In a world where crossing boundaries is routine, CQ becomes a vitally important aptitude and skill. Cultural intelligence is an extension of emotional intelligence. A person with high EQ grasps what makes us human and at the same time what makes each of us different from one another. A person with high CQ can somehow discern from the behaviour of a person or group those features that would be true of all people and all groups, those peculiar to this person or this group, and those that are neither universal nor idiosyncratic.

In common with emotional intelligence there are three sources of cultural intelligence: the head, heart and body. The head involves learning about the beliefs, customs and taboos of foreign cultures. However, this will never prepare you for every situation that arises; nor will it prevent interpersonal errors. The body builds on learning about other cultures by demonstrating to yourself and others personal learning through action, for example by greeting people in the custom of their own country. Consider for example the ways that the people of the different countries of Europe greet each other on meeting, from the somewhat distant reserve of the British to the more formal, effusive nature of the French. Providing evidence of an ability to mirror the customs and gestures of the people around you proves that you value them well enough to want to be like them. And you eventually come to understand what it is to be them. In turn, they will become more trusting and open in their relationship with you, which is good for conducting business and developing networks. The final area to consider in developing CQ is the heart. Adapting to a new culture involves overcoming obstacles and setbacks, which requires strong belief to persist in the face of potentially challenging situations. A person who does not believe themselves capable of understanding people from unfamiliar cultures will often give up after their efforts meet with hostility or incomprehension. Consider, for example, how challenging it is communicating in a foreign country with a limited knowledge of the language. Consequently, to communicate verbally and non-verbally, through the responses and actions of the body, requires strong, personal motivation.

For health care leaders working across Europe, cultural intelligence will grow to be as important as emotional intelligence to the personal development of good leadership. This is for the following interconnected contextual reasons that were discussed in Chapter 3:

- the increasingly converging health and health care leadership and management agendas of the countries of Europe;
- the increasing influence of the European Union on the future organisation of health care across Europe;
- the increasing movement of the professional workforce across Europe for employment and postgraduate training purposes;
- the growing impact of consumerism and increasing patient mobility.

This European-wide context will result in increasing contact between individual countries at a number of levels: political, policy development, mutual learning about policy implementation, and planning for workforce and patient movement. Consequently, cultural intelligence, learning to communicate in and understand each other's cultures, will be important. However, in common with emotional intelligence, cultural intelligence can also be developed by personal training and practice based on personal reflection and self-awareness.

EQ AND LEADERSHIP TEAMS

Leading high-performing teams

When teams work together effectively they achieve their strategic intentions and objectives much more quickly, for example by extending the capabilities of the leader of the team and by helping themselves and those around them to make sense of context and ambiguous, sometimes contradictory data. Also, they are much more likely to work through and survive difficult times. The main challenge for teams is not being seen as a team in name only because they have failed to develop and apply the team's collective skills. The potential pitfalls for teams include team members' protecting their functional areas of responsibility, being misguided in their thinking about leadership by abdicating personal leadership roles, considering themselves immune from the culture and behaviour of the rest of the organisation, and failing to put in sufficient work on process to make the team work effectively.

The leader of a team may have a background in operational or clinical management or a functional area such as accounting. If the leader has self-awareness then they will eventually realise that their experience and achievements will eventually become out-of-date and less relevant to their overall leadership role. Consequently, they will require sufficient self-awareness to acknowledge the need to increasingly rely on the skills, experience, knowledge and networks of other team members. This is particularly so when the leader is new in post. Sometimes, insisting on gender and ethnic diversity is the only way to ensure that a team considers a wide range of options and opinions. Above all, the most important thing is to avoid all-male leadership cultures because women tend to have stronger empathy and relationship skills than men do, which is important not only for team working but also in establishing effective networks between the team and wider stakeholders. Men can of course exhibit these skills too just as women can demonstrate toughness and decisiveness when required. When there is sufficient trust on a leadership team, gender diversity can boost the team's ability to manage its own emotions and respond to those of others. To lead and develop a team of effective, successful individuals, create high levels of team energy and capitalise on the skills of team members you will need to focus on the following sixfold process:

1 articulate a clear vision for the future because all teams need clear aims and objectives to measure their progress and success;
2 ideally, select only team members whose experience is required to achieve the team's objectives, excluding those with duplicate skills and removing those who are not team players;

115

3 at regular intervals review team processes and procedures to see whether they are advancing or hindering team efforts;

4 when reviewing progress maintain a strong focus on strategy, do not lapse into discussing tactics with the consequential risk of losing strategic focus;

5 create a climate for trust and integrity so that team members can express their views openly, including dissent when required, and engage in positive discussion of ideas;

6 give individual and group feedback at good times and bad, and reward team members, for example by providing personal development opportunities for future career progression.

Groupthink

The majority of people will spend most of their working lives interacting with other people. Chief executives, directors, heads of services and others in leadership positions will have to lead teams, influence networks and stakeholders within and outside their service or organisation, as well as manage upwards to ensure ongoing organisational and/or political support for their plans. As has been stated above, teams tend to be more productive when they achieve high levels of participation, cooperation and collaboration. These behaviours are not always easy to establish because they require the development of effective interpersonal relationships and trust, at the heart of which is emotion. It is only by being honest with each other about challenges and feelings about challenges, coupled with providing support to each other at times of difficulty, that teams can build trust and take risks in pursuing their objectives. However, one of the risks for leadership team working is the development of 'groupthink' or a bunker mentality (Bass 1990). Groupthink explains why highly competent members of a group sometimes can make poor collective decisions. Why this happens is often because the group is very cohesive and a unanimous view is formed solely out of a sense of mutual loyalty to themselves. The signs of groupthink include:

- aggressive pressure on those who disagree with the team;
- one-sided discussions dismissing competition and alternative views;
- stopping listening to others such as frontline staff, external stakeholders and consumers.

The inevitable malfunctioning of the team will also result in the blurring of strategic focus and a reduction in performance as team objectives are not met in terms of timescale or outcomes. One way to counteract groupthink is to make sure the leadership team comprises diverse styles and perspectives. Consequently, the more experienced, wise and mature leaders will know that they have to surround themselves with people who have the personal skills and knowledge to think differently and undertake tasks that the leader finds difficult or does not have the skills to achieve. Strong teams also manage emotion across the wider organisation, network or system by communicating in a timely and wise fashion, particularly at times of stress and difficulty in achieving objectives. They will listen to outside views particularly from staff, other stakeholders and consumers, and nurture external relationships particularly across networks. If you want to improve the emotional intelligence of your team, then you need to start by changing your own behaviour whether you are a team member or the team's leader. Your willingness to acknowledge and discuss emotions can start a team's development of its emotional intelligence. Further, develop the EQ skills of others via communication courses, individual coaching, training and development and formal appraisals. To summarise, teams will use emotional intelligence to increase their effectiveness and build the awareness of the feelings of team members by:

1   Regularly taking a holistic contextual perspective, which means looking at situations and challenges from the viewpoint of other team members. This will help ensure the team 'manages the future' as much as possible and does not feel powerless or overrun by events.

2   Maintaining interpersonal understanding, which means ensuring that team members know each other well so that they are alert to mood changes. This would include showing care and concern for the feelings and personal circumstances of team members, for example noticing when a team member is upset for personal reasons.

3   Allowing team members to confront each other's unacceptable behaviour without damaging self-respect.

4   Introducing humour to lighten mood or challenge odd behaviour, for example, lightly commenting to a team member who is routinely late for meetings shows the importance of punctuality and also highlights a breach of team rules.

5   Achieving objectives and solving problems when they arise, which increases the team's sense of self-worth and value. Nothing motivates and increases self-worth likes success.

6   Self-evaluating the team's corporate performance in order to review effectiveness and help build team spirit.

7 Obtaining feedback from others within and outside the organisation or network, possibly using a 360° process so that the team is seen to be open to constructive criticism.

8 Developing a 'can-do' attitude, for example by endeavouring to be optimistic in outlook.

The above reflects the importance of teams agreeing the norms for how they will work together. To give one example, the national Top Team for managing the NHS for England has collectively agreed that it will work according to the following principles, which are displayed around the room at every meeting:

THE NHS IN ENGLAND: TOP TEAM VALUES AND RULES

Values
The work of the Top Team should be based on the following values:

- Lead not blame
- Work together not undermine each other
- Look for answers not give excuses
- Put the patient and public at the centre of our work

Simple Rules
- Collectively give authority to team members to act and let them deliver
- Aim for agreement (wherever possible) and stick to it
- Aim for honest closure where we cannot agree
- Speak well of each other – inside and outside meetings
- Try our hardest to work on a 'no surprises' basis
- Involve each other as early as possible

LEADING CHANGE THROUGH EMOTIONS

Personal stress

Too little or too much stress is bad for us in the long term. In everyday normal stressful situations, the experience is often pleasurable because we survive the threat. In simple terms, stress is an aspect of living that can be beneficial when it motivates, encourages change or inspires. When it does not do any of these things then distress can occur because individuals see that they do not have the resources to cope with a situation from the past, present or future. More often than not when people complain about stressful situations, it is because of a feeling of tension or pressure experienced when demands placed upon them are seen as exceeding the personal skills or resources they have available. The most common symptom is that people do not feel well and medical practitioners can find no clinical reason. In the Stone Age there would have been a physical response to these symptoms in fighting or running away from the danger. In the modern world, the body response is the same but the threats we see are of a financial, emotional, mental and a social nature. These types of threats are ever present in our personal and professional lives and are not generally dealt with quickly.

Being regularly stressed causes illness because the stress will begin to prevent relaxation or proper sleep for the body or mind to repair itself. In organisations the negative effects of stress can be seen in poor-quality decision-making, deteriorating interpersonal relationships, poor policy formulation and poorly thought through reactions to policy, reduced creativity and individual apathy. Hallowell (2005) has identified attention deficit trait (ADT), which is caused by brain overload and he argues is endemic in organisations. The core symptoms are distractibility, inner frenzy and impatience, which results in individuals staying organised, determining priorities and managing their time. The symptoms of ADT, which are precipitated by the working environment, come upon a person gradually rather than because of a single crisis. In the light of increasing inner panic about objectives to be met, the individual becomes increasingly hurried, curt and unfocused while pretending that everything is fine. In other words, the person becomes more and more stressed. Leaders have a responsibility to ensure that stress in themselves and their staff is acknowledged and managed positively. Asking people to do too much without adequate support is a common problem as organisations, including those in health care, endeavour to control costs by, among other things, reducing or eliminating middle-management tiers in organisational hierarchies. Leaders can help reduce ADT by not only looking after themselves and minimising the transfer of their personal stress to others, but also by matching staff skills to the objectives to be achieved. A mismatch between the two will potentially precipitate stress. At an organisational level, Hallowell (ibid.) cites the US company SAS Institute, which offers its staff a range of support services including a gym, a day-care facility, unlimited sick days and a seven-hour workday that ends at 5p.m.

Emotional intelligence should also be used to manage stress by managing relationships, environment, lifestyle and attitude and reactions. Associating with those whose company we enjoy and who provide support generally allows us to have authentic, emotionally intelligent relationships with other people both professionally and personally. In common with most organisations, health care organisations work through interconnected systems of interpersonal relationships, which continually reminds us that people do business with other people, whether in their own organisation or across intra- or inter-organisational networks. Consequently, we prefer to seek out people we enjoy doing business with and try to avoid those people with whom we find it harder to establish interpersonal relationships. To help minimise the risk of personal stress we should, if at all possible, try not to associate with people who drain our emotional batteries by creating unacceptable anxiety and conflict. However, in our professional lives achieving that can be difficult or often impossible. Consequently, we need to learn how to have assertive conversations with those who create anxiety in ourselves. We should try not to drift along in troublesome and distressing situations or relationships and we should learn to be assertive and to take control of difficult situations. Coaching and mentoring are important sources of support and establishing a co-coaching relationship with someone we trust can help develop tactics and strategies for learning to prepare for and manage stress situations (coaching is discussed further in Chapter 7).

Maintaining positive emotions

If there is considerable uncertainty generated about a change being pursued then it will put the leader under intense scrutiny and often bring hidden emotions to the surface. If people do not appear comfortable in leading change then nagging doubts will emerge in both the leader and those around them. There are however, four ways for a leader to demonstrate through personal behaviour that the change being led is an opportunity rather than being seen as a major risk, potential setback or potential failure:

1   Let go of the past
    We cannot change what has already happened so continually dwelling on past events, other than for personal and group learning purposes, is counter-productive.

2   Maintain focus
    Keep a strong personal focus by ensuring that discussions you have with your team and other key players stay firmly on the future and where you are going, not where you have been. It is important not to hang onto to past issues and processes, because if you – as the leader – do not move forward with new processes and ways of doing things, no one else will.

3   Dispel doubt

Do not dwell on any doubts and even if you have them, do not let them surface. The confidence that you display about the future is important in the eyes of others. If you express doubts about the future direction, other than undertaking an objective risk assessment of the plan for how to get there, then others will be infected by your uncertainty.

4   Maintain visibility

Stay visible and keep connected to the proposed change. Although many leaders get tired of having to constantly reassure others, by keeping in touch you will be able to quickly respond to rumours, address doubts and provide positive reinforcement for the changes underway. Developing a network of trusted colleagues is a good way of keeping in touch with the feelings and views across wider networks.

At times of change leaders need to recognise and manage their own anxiety. Being self-aware of your own emotions is as important as being aware of the emotions of those of your team and in the wider networks around you. It is common for leadership teams involved in a change programme to positively support their staff by providing personal support and counselling, inviting discussion and constructive comment, and empathising strongly with the almost inevitable range of positive and negative emotions generated at times of change. However, they then fail to support themselves and each other. Admitting fear or anxiety can be viewed as acceptable for middle managers and junior staff but not permissible for high-level leadership teams, senior executives or board directors. The potential adverse consequence for leaders and senior executives not managing their emotions is that the leadership team becomes exhausted, anxious and stressed, with the result that they are likely to be seen by others as the single most important obstacle to a successful outcome. This does not mean that leaders should not display their emotions or indeed discuss their weaknesses as a way of showing their human side. But care needs to be exercised because this does not mean displaying complete openness and discretion is required about when and what to disclose. Leaders do need to admit mistakes because like everyone else they are fallible and this helps establish trust and generate support from followers for their vision of the future. When leaders reveal their weaknesses, they are displaying to others who they really are.

If leaders try to communicate that they are perfect at everything then there would be no need for anyone to help them with anything. They will not need followers and they are signalling that they can do it all themselves. But displaying or admitting to weakness must be done carefully: it will do no good to admit to indecisiveness at difficult times, for example when people will be expecting firm leadership and support. Good leaders own up to selective weaknesses but knowing which weakness to disclose requires careful consideration (Goffee and Jones 2000). The rule to follow is never to expose a weakness that will be seen as a fatal flaw. This may mean admitting an interpersonal weakness such as being irritable first thing in the morning or perhaps being rather shy when in large groups. Such admissions work because people need to see leaders own up to some flaw before they participate willingly in following them. Another approach is to identify a weakness that can in some ways be considered strength such as being a workaholic. When leaders expose these limited flaws, others will not see much of anything and little harm will be done to them. However if the leader's vulnerability is not perceived to be genuine then they will not gain anyone's support. Instead, they will open themselves up to ridicule and scorn and their followers will quickly drift away. Finally, at the same time as revealing themselves as human, leaders also need to reassure and provide constancy, clarity and support to those around them. This may require leaders absorbing the emotional outpourings of staff, while appearing to remain in control of their own emotions. Consequently, they need to find other ways and places to pour out their own feelings. This can be done with those most trusted and closest to the leader, such as members of their own family, executive team or with a mentor or coach.

Finally, remember that leaders' moods affect the emotions of the people around them. The reason for that lies in the open-loop nature of the limbic system, the brain's emotional centre. A closed-loop system is self-regulating, whereas an open-loop system depends on external sources to manage itself. In other words, we rely on connections with other people to determine our moods. The limbic system's open-loop design lets other people change our emotions and hence people 'catch' feelings from one another in their work. Groups, in common with individuals, take emotional journeys every day sharing everything from jealousy to angst to euphoria. Of practical importance to leaders is the knowledge that of all emotions, laughter is the most contagious. Hearing laughter, people find it almost impossible not to laugh or smile too. That is because some of the brain's open-loop circuits are designed to detect smiles and laughter, making us respond in kind. The main implication here for leaders wanting to manage their own moods and those of others is that humour hastens the spread of an upbeat climate. However, like the leader's mood in general, humour must resonate with the organisation's culture and its reality. Consequently, smiles and laughter are only contagious when they are genuine.

Finally, the limbic brain is a much slower learner than the neocortex, the thinking part of the brain. This is significant because most personal development for emotional intelligence abilities, such as leadership, focus on the latter rather than the former. Because our feelings, impulses and drives are learnt early in life, learning new ways of managing these emotions takes longer and in general, success is dependent on lots of practice and repetition. Personal leadership development is discussed further in Chapter 7.

CONCLUSION

We live and work in a world that is driven by emotions. Emotional issues often drive us; such as fear of loss of face, the need for reassurance or the inner desire for control. Consequently, we need to be emotionally literate, which means understanding the emotional forces around and within all of us, not in order to parade them around the organisation but to contain them appropriately and learn from them. An emotionally literate workplace is not one where everyone is in tears or hugging each other all the time. It is one where people are sufficiently emotionally stable so that they can get on with their jobs, rather than using the organisation as a personal stage for openly discussing the unresolved issues of lives outside work. Organisations and their leaders need to recognise that emotions play an important and growing role in public life. In developed, affluent countries, satisfaction with life is much more strongly related to soft variables such as intimate relationships, intrinsic job satisfaction and companionship than to hard indicators like pay and position. Everybody has emotional issues that define him or her and shape their personal and professional behaviour. The challenge is to take the development of emotional skills seriously. To summarise, the emotionally intelligent person is skilled in four areas: identifying emotions, understanding emotions, using emotions and regulating emotions. To achieve that requires three essential personal skills:

1   Knowing what you are feeling, and being able to handle those feelings without them wholly dominating your interpersonal relationships and decision-making.
2   Being able to motivate yourself to achieve personal and group objectives, to be innovative and creative, and to perform at your peak.
3   Sensing what your team and others in wider networks are feeling and handling interpersonal and inter-organisational relationships effectively.

DISCUSSION QUESTIONS

1 Are you aware of your emotions at work, your emotional strengths and weaknesses, how you behave in different situations and your impact on people around you?

2 Are you able to regulate your emotions, to build on your behavioural strengths and change any aspect of your personal behaviour if that is necessary? If you need help to do these things do you know how to access that, for example from a close colleague or executive coach?

3 Are you aware of the emotions of members of your team and others around you? Do you know what they are feeling in different situations and at different times and why?

4 Are you able to stay composed under stress? If not, do you know where and how to obtain support to help you achieve that?

5 Are you able to positively confront difficult behaviour or stressful situations within your team, organisation or across your networks?

6 Do you understand gut instinct? Are you able to listen to and understand what your 'three brains' (head, heart and gut) are saying to you at times of difficulty or stress?

7 Are you able to seek feedback from others on the impact of both your current and changed behaviours in order to improve your leadership?

BIBLIOGRAPHY AND FURTHER READING

Bass B.M. (1990) *Bass and Stogdill's Handbook of Leadership Theory, Research and Managerial Applications*. New York: The Free Press.

Cooper R.K. (2000) A new neuroscience of leadership: bringing out more of the best in people. *Strategy and Leadership* (28)6: 11–15.

Earley P.C. and Mosakowski E. (2004) Cultural intelligence. *Harvard Business Review* October: 139–146.

Goffee R. and Jones G. (2000) Why should anyone be led by you? *Harvard Business Review* September–October: 62–70.

Goleman D. (1998) *Working with Emotional Intelligence*. London: Bloomsbury.

Goleman R., Boyatzis R. and McKee A. (2001) Primal leadership: the hidden driver of great performance. *Harvard Business Review* December: 42–51.

Goleman R., Boyatzis R. and McKee A. (2002) *Primal Leadership. Realizing the power of emotional intelligence*. Boston, MA: Harvard Business School Publishing.

Hallowell E.M. (2005) Why smart people underperform. *Harvard Business Review* January Special Issue: 55–62.

Hayashi A.M. (2001) When to Trust your Gut. *Harvard Business Review* February: 59–65.

Chapter 6

Health care leadership in action

KEY POINTS OF THIS CHAPTER

- Health care management is heavily context driven and a case-study research approach provides a frame of reference for both the researcher and the reader to interpret events.
- The research results presented here are relevant to all health care organisations across Europe.
- Successful leadership involves achieving a balance between implementing nationally driven change and achieving objectives seen as significant to local players.
- Successful leaders need the support of an able team, and networks of other leaders and followers both within and across health care organisational boundaries.

KEY TERMS

- UK National Health Service (NHS)
- National and local context
- Primary care group (PCG)
- General practitioner (GP)
- Local medical committee (LMC)
- Local government authorities
- Case study

- Qualitative research
- Organisational boundaries
- Network and networking

INTRODUCTION

The previous two chapters on networks and emotional intelligence began the discussion of how leadership is undertaken. As a reminder, the emergence of a network-based approach to leadership, underpinned by a growing interest in the importance of emotional intelligence, reflects the preoccupation of the last century with leadership tasks being replaced by an emphasis on people issues such as pursuing mutual purposes and establishing reciprocal leader–follower relations. Consequently, successful leadership is dependent on understanding context and developing a network of successful interpersonal and inter-organisational relationships in order to secure agreement for moving forward with change. As such, leadership is not a series of single actions but a process of continual interaction with the environment and other people within the organisation and beyond. We have also seen that leadership is not an isolated activity and the creation and successful management of leadership teams is important along with acknowledging and managing emotions and risk. Finally, we need to acknowledge that leadership is not always successful and failure – for both the organisation and the leader – can happen (failure is discussed in detail in Chapter 7).

This chapter builds on the theme of the two previous chapters by discussing how leadership is practised. The aim of the chapter is to bring to life how leadership is undertaken in differing contexts by presenting the results of a major qualitative research study into chief executive leadership in England and then considering how the results would apply across Europe (Goodwin 2002). The chapter also outlines the background and approach to the research not only for the benefit of the general reader but also because it may be helpful to students of management who are considering undertaking similar research.

THE ENGLISH NATIONAL HEALTH SERVICE

The English National Health Service (NHS) is a large and complex organisation comprising a number of parts and groups connected in different ways and from different perspectives: political, managerial, clinical, local and national.

In less than two decades various UK governments and their ideologies have changed the organisation of the NHS. It has shifted from a hierarchical, administrative structure with multi-disciplinary management teams operating by consensus; through a system that replaced central planning and nationally determined structures with a private sector, internal market model with general management and chief executives; to today's system that developed following the election of the 1997 Labour government. Labour's 1997 proposals retained much of the previous arrangements but replaced the historically fragmented purchasing structure with primary care groups, for the first time bringing all general practitioners (namely primary care physicians) into the corporate management hierarchy of the NHS. It also replaced the competition-based market of the early 1990s with an approach based on collaboration and partnership coupled with a strengthened governmental role in determining national policies, operational standards and strategies. In the last two years, the government has introduced policies based on greater consumer choice and pluralism in the provision of services by, among other things, encouraging greater state use of UK and international independent health care providers. In 2004 NHS hospitals also could apply to become 'foundation hospitals'. These are non-NHS bodies providing NHS services but with considerable organisational freedom and accountable to an independent regulator rather like the UK's power and water public utility companies. Collectively, this raft of policies are an extension of the market-driven model favoured by the previous Conservative government, which also is to be supported by a new financial regime currently being introduced (Department of Health 2004). In addition, the government has signalled its intention to introduce general practice-based commissioning, which will see practices holding indicative budgets for purchasing health care for their patients coupled with the ability to retain savings.

The 1997 Labour government inherited the historical and seemingly intractable problems of the English NHS, namely a conflict of priorities plus a continuing and permanent excess of demand over supply for health care. For health care managers, who have to come to terms with a reality different from the ideology of politicians, this means having to make choices that both advantage and disadvantage their local populations, which can result in seemingly continual conflict and controversy. Perhaps also like previous governments, particularly the successive Conservative administrations of 1979 to 1997, Labour concluded that the failure of NHS management to deliver a comprehensive and consumer-sensitive NHS reflected a failure of leadership within the NHS. At the heart of the Labour government's approach since 1997 is the importance of public sector stewardship and values. Although these have implications for the style of public sector and NHS management, Labour's policies for the NHS were launched without clear consideration of the management style required to support them. Perhaps not surprisingly, in 1999 government ministers called for a leadership drive to create NHS managers with the skills to work in a collaborative and involving way.

The Labour government's plans were set out in its policy, *The New NHS. Modern. Dependable* (Department of Health 1997). Although the purchaser–provider split established by the previous Conservative government was maintained, general practitioner (GP) fundholding (namely the 1990 system of individual GPs holding budgets to purchase local health services for their patients) was abolished although as indicated in the previous paragraph, a form of it is currently being introduced as practice-based commissioning. Fundholding for GPs was the most visible manifestation of the former internal market. In its place primary care groups (PCGs) were introduced, which were seen as the cornerstone of the government's change programme for the NHS because unlike fundholding, the groups formally engaged all GPs in the corporate management of the NHS for the first time in its history. It is the introduction of the groups that forms the basis of the research presented here. Each group was responsible to the local health authority for purchasing health care for an average 100,000 population. Other aspects of Labour's policies included a requirement for health authorities to develop three-year health improvement programmes and targeting £100m of annual savings from management costs. The accountability of NHS chief executives was also enhanced with the creation of clinical governance, which placed the responsibility for the quality of health care on hospital chief executives. Two new bodies, the National Institute for Clinical Excellence (NICE) and the Commission for Health Improvement (CHI) were introduced. The role of NICE was to ensure equal standards and treatment availability across the country, while CHI's job was to monitor service improvements. The role of CHI was extended in 2004 and the organisation renamed the Healthcare Commission.

Labour's big idea for the NHS did not come until it was three years into power: an idea that was simply stated. After keeping the health budget on a tight rein for its first two to three years the government was to expand it hugely. A second NHS plan, *A plan for investment, a plan for reform* (Department of Health 2000), announced an historic commitment to a sustained increase in NHS spending to bring it into line with the European average. Too often, the report said, patients had to wait too long, while variations in standards across the country were unacceptable. Constraints on funding mean that staff often work under great pressure and lack the time and resources they need to offer the best possible service, the plan added. Further strands of policy have emerged since then that focus on: patient choice and personalisation of health care, which includes NHS Direct – a 24-hour telephone and internet advice service; walk-in centres available for 365 days a year; proposals to provide each patient with their own electronic 'health space' where they can record personal information about their health and lifestyle; and from the end of 2004, offering all patients who have waited more than six months for hospital treatment a choice of alternative hospital, including independent sector alternatives (Department of Health 2004). Finally, a new performance target has been announced: by December 2008 the maximum waiting time for referral from primary care to treatment in secondary care is to be 18 weeks. Achieving this target would represent a dramatic achievement in the performance of the English NHS. In reality, the UK government has started to engage in a large-scale financial and mixed market experiment. The test during future years is whether the UK NHS can respond to an enormous increase in funding by dramatically improving access to health care as represented by the 2008 target.

THE RESEARCH AND THE RESULTS

Background to the research

The qualitative, case study-based research summarised in this chapter explored leadership as a social phenomenon using as its basis the implementation of the primary care group policy in four health authorities across England. Government implementation guidance made it clear that health authority chief executives were accountable for implementing the primary care group policy locally. At the time the research fieldwork was undertaken in the late 1990s health authority chief executives were establishing primary care groups and preparing to delegate power and responsibility to them. As such, they were required to consult with a wide range of local NHS and other stakeholders, such as local (municipal) government, in order to secure consensus agreement to the size and number of groups.

Forming the basis of the research were 141 semi-structured interviews along with a review of relevant documentation such as government policies, and health authority plans and correspondence. The interviews were carried out across four English health authorities, their emerging primary care groups and local (municipal) government authorities, the UK department of health, central government, and national GP representative organisations such as the British Medical Association. Personal and organisational success for each chief executive was defined as securing agreement from local players to an acceptable geographical configuration of primary care groups within their local health systems. In reality the number per health authority ranged from four to twelve. The research did not assess the question of the longer-term success or otherwise of the groups once they had been established. Since the groups have been established, English NHS history shows they have been replaced by primary care trusts, which unlike their predecessors, are free-standing statutory organisations with responsibility for commissioning local health services, performance monitoring local health care providers and establishing inter-agency partnerships to improve local population health.

Importantly, the research approach presented here embraces the historical criticisms of leadership research referred to in Chapter 1, namely that there has been too much focus on the peripheries of leadership such as traits and personality characteristics or on the management of whole organisations. Consequently, there has been insufficient exploration of two interrelated issues: the nature of leadership as a process or dynamic relationship and the reciprocal relationship between leadership and context. In addition, as was seen in Chapter 2, the numerous leadership movements and models that have emerged historically are presented separately and distinctly when in fact they too are interrelated. Consequently, to properly explore organisational and inter-organisational leadership in the context of the political and open system-based management of public services, a broad and holistic contextual approach is required. For these reasons a qualitative, rather than quantitative, research approach was adopted. The main objective of qualitative studies is to describe the variation in a phenomenon, situation or attitude, whereas quantitative research is limited to quantifying the variation (Kumar 1999). Others supporting this include Smircich and Morgan (1982), and Bresnen (1995) who argues that what is required is a more interpretative approach, complemented by appropriate qualitative research techniques. This is in order to explore in greater depth the meaning of leadership and the relationship between processes occurring at social and psychological levels. In addition, a case study approach offers the strengths of experimental research within natural settings (Hakim 1987) and the opportunity for the intensive analysis of many specific details often overlooked by other methods (Kumar ibid.). Since the literature shows health care management being heavily context driven, the case study approach allows the context to be a major emphasis during the research and provides a frame of reference for both the researcher and the reader to interpret events (Mitchell 1983; Bryman 1989).

The literature and background to the research raised a number of possible research questions against the backdrop of government-driven change programmes that have been a regular feature of life for the English NHS and its senior leadership for the last 25 years. For example, is it nationally and externally driven change, such as government policies and targets, rather than individuals that primarily account for organisational performance across local health care services? Can it be determined under what contextual conditions chief executives and other leaders of local health care services can make a difference and what distinguishes those who can from those who cannot? If there is a distinguishing feature is it leadership that is the unique factor? Further, if national bodies such as governments or insurance funds are seen as generators of constraints, largely because they determine resource availability for health systems, then is it the ability of local chief executives and their teams to turn constraints into positive opportunities that differentiates them by turning managers into leaders? These questions, which flowed from the review of the literature, were distilled into three research propositions, which formed the basis of the research across the four English health authorities:

1   The operating environment or context is different and its successful management is important to personal and organisational success for health care system leaders.
2   Health authorities have become externally focused network-based organisations, which is important to personal and organisational success for health system leaders.
3   Health system leadership is rooted in achieving a balance between implementing nationally driven policy (such as that from government) and achieving locally driven significant objectives, which taken together constitute overall organisational and personal success for health system leaders.

These research questions and the results presented below are relevant to most health care organisations across Europe for the following three reasons. First, European health care is heavily context-driven by governments, social insurance funds, national and regional politics, and more locally by clinicians and the public as consumers. Understanding and distilling the messages from differing national and local contexts is a core leadership skill. Second, the evolving nature of health care organisations, delivery of health care and the pursuance of improved population health increasingly requires leadership and management to be conducted in a relationship with other health care and non-health care organisations. Third, the general principles and practices of leadership and management are the same the world over and it is only country-based contextual and cultural differences that influence how they are pursued in detail.

THE STORY OF FOUR CHIEF EXECUTIVES

The national context for the research

Regarding the national environment, interviewees in each of the four health systems were generally positive and supportive of the government's broad policy approach and the more specific policy to introduce primary care groups. However, the four chief executives and general practitioners speculated negatively about the government's longer-term vision and strategy. Some were suspicious about whether there was a hidden agenda of greater governmental control of the medical profession. Players linked both policy formulation and its implementation in their interviews. In contrast to their positive views about the content of government NHS policy there was overwhelming negativity about the government's style and speed of policy implementation. This was primarily because of concern about the time needed to develop local support for change. The majority of views were also negative about governmental guidance for implementing primary care groups because they saw it as too detailed and prescriptive, failing to provide sufficient discretion for chief executives to take into account local context in its implementation. These views about the role of government reflect the findings of previous public sector management research, namely concerns about the artificiality of time constraints, the lack of influence over government policy formulation and the need to implement managerial agendas within a highly politicised context. So on one level there appears to be little, if anything, new from the research results presented here. However, what is different and will be demonstrated is that leadership is possible in such an environment.

Although the four chief executives implemented the primary care group policy on time and in a way acceptable to government, the local contextual issues were not only different but also considerable. Analysis showed each health authority chief executive having a number of important local challenges focusing on strategy formulation and decision-making, financial control and establishing effective inter-organisational working relationships. In the context of national politics, the four health authorities had been trying to bring these issues to a conclusion over time periods longer than the electoral cycles of individual national governments. The research results showed that each chief executive pursued implementation in both hierarchical and non-hierarchical ways. For example, one health authority incorporated the new primary care groups into its existing hierarchical, committee-based management structure, while another grafted the groups onto its already established, decentralised, non-hierarchical GP-led commissioning groups.

To successfully implement the PCG policy the four chief executives had to secure the support of a number of external players (summarised for the four health systems in Table 6.1.) The stakeholder literature says that a more successful outcome is probable if it is clear at the start which players are more significant than others in terms of influencing the shape of the future. For the four chief executives these players were:

- general practitioners because they were to lead the new primary care groups;
- local medical committees because they represent the professional interests of GPs locally;
- local government authorities (similar to municipal authorities) because they were to be represented on PCGs and have a bigger role in local health issues generally;
- NHS Trusts because as providers of secondary health care they consume the vast majority of local resources and as such are powerful players.

What follows is a summary of how each chief executive approached implementation of the primary care group policy, drawing out lessons about management, leadership, networks and networking. The four chief executives are referred to as chief executive 1, chief executive 2, chief executive 3 and chief executive 4.

Table 6.1 *Number of players per local health system by organisation*

Organisation	Number of players per health system			
	1	2	3	4
NHS Trusts[1]	3	4	4	10
General practitioners (GPs)[2]	184	276	347	583
GP practices[3]	46	74	119	244
Local government authorities[4]	2	2	5	1
Local medical committees (LMCs)[5]	1	1	1	1

1 Providers of secondary health care services, mainly hospitals.
2 Primary care physicians, independent contractors to the NHS; they act as gatekeepers to secondary care services.
3 The number of practices within which the GPs have organised themselves for work.
4 The local democratically elected body led by local politicians, provides municipal services such as environmental health, education and social care.
5 The professional representative body for GPs, similar to a trade union.

Chief executive 1

Chief executive 1 led a mainly urban health system centering on a major provincial city in the north of England. Historically, the chief executive had taken an opportunistic approach in 1994 to engage disaffected general practitioners in the corporate management of the health authority because of their unhappiness over the closure of their favourite hospital as a result of a strategic review of acute hospital services. The chief executive's approach involved the appointment of a former GP as health authority director of primary care, who was appointed with the remit to network across the local health system and re-engage general practitioners in the work of the health authority. The director successfully led the establishment of GP commissioning groups thereby integrating them into health authority decision-making of future health care strategy. The actions of the director established the beginnings of a network-based organisation for the chief executive and his team. For networks to be effective the personal reputation of those leading them is important and the research results confirmed that local players, particularly GPs, held the director of primary in high personal regard.

When commenting on the leadership style of the health authority 'facilitative' and 'discursive' were words used by local stakeholders to describe both the organisation and its chief executive. In contrast with the other three chief executives, chief executive 1 did not have a high profile outside the organisation but was said in a positive way by local players, to 'lead from behind' using a devolved leadership style. The leadership style of chief executive 1 in terms of acting through an intermediary was also used by chief executive 4 who pursued implementation of the primary care group policy via the GP-led local medical committee rather than dealing directly with GPs. However, the difference between the two chief executives was that this was not chief executive 4's natural style: he had a higher external profile than chief executive 1 but recognised that the local medical committee had a stronger reputation with GPs than he and his own organisation. The approach of these two chief executives reflects the tactic of acting through intermediaries in order to help implement change. However, chief executive 1's approach did not mean abrogating personal involvement from the leadership process and associated decision-making. He had a clear view of the desired outcome and became directly involved when implementation difficulties arose.

By the time chief executive 1 introduced primary care groups effective networks with local GPs and local government had been established for a few years. The strength and effectiveness of these interpersonal and inter-organisational networks were seen by local players to have assisted implementing the primary care group policy, particularly networks between the health authority and local GP leaders and in turn, the latter's networks with local GP colleagues. Consequently, implementation of the primary care group policy was seen by local players and government to have been smooth. In the light of the chief executive's devolved approach to leadership, players confirmed in the research interviews the strategic importance and strength of the chief executive's executive team in leading the local health care system.

Chief executive 1 was not successful in all aspects of the implementation. First, in response to pressure from local GPs he could not secure from national government greater flexibility for the primary care group governance arrangements. This however did not sour local relationships and the chief executive resolved the matter by adopting a flexible interpretation of the governance rules. Two further implementation problems faced by the chief executive involved the management of difficult groups of players. A proposal from the health system's former GP fundholders to form their own, separate primary care group was firmly rejected on the basis that the proposed geographical configuration of the proposed group was unworkable. Again the health authority's director of primary care took a lead role in the process of resolving the tension, and non-fundholding local GPs and the chief executive supported him in that. The second problem was a request from some GPs to establish what would be a very small primary care group in terms of population and numbers of GPs. In this case however, the chief executive supported the proposal because it was his judgement that although creating a small primary care group was unlikely to be sustainable this was not an issue requiring immediate resolution. There were two thoughts uppermost in the mind of the chief executive when he granted the request. First, given the history of local relationships with general practitioners he did not want to completely reject a second request from the key players whose support he needed to make the groups work. And second, the proposed group would be led by a GP who was a powerful member of the local medical committee. The apparent quid pro quo between the chief executive and local GPs – their support for his decision against the former GP fundholders in return for establishing the smaller primary care group – reflects the management literature in that overcoming individual idiosyncrasies or dealing with egos is important to successful collaboration with stakeholders.

The actions of chief executive 1 reflect clear moves to establish his health system on a network basis and to exercise leadership in tackling both significant local challenges and implementing externally driven change. In summary, the key components of the chief executive's approach to the management of the local health care system and implementation of the primary care group policy were:

- Building on a history of sustainable relationships with local general practitioners created after a major disagreement over strategy for local acute hospital services.
- Demonstrating a commitment to change the status quo by historically devolving power and budgets to GPs well before the primary care group policy was introduced; in other words anticipating the future.
- Developing networks and networking to build relationships with local GP leaders and organisations to, among other things, help implement the primary care group policy.
- Operating through an effective executive team with complementary skills, knowledge and experience, that was viewed positively by local players.
- Making political and pragmatic judgements about local implementation issues that were generally supported by local players.
- Re-interpreting implementation aspects of externally driven national proposals for change in order to secure local acceptance and support.

Chief executive 2

Chief executive 2 led a semi-rural health system based on two towns in eastern England. In general terms chief executive 2's managerial control, and strategy formulation and implementation are in complete contrast to the other three chief executives. General practitioner support for the primary care group policy was pursued against a backdrop of major local financial, strategic and inter-organisational relationship challenges that had been present for many years. Players interviewed for the research argued that many of the problems were as a direct result of the lack of managerial control and leadership of the local health system by the chief executive and his team.

The chief executive's approach to introducing primary care groups built on his previous initiative to formally incorporate all GPs into five fundholding-based groups responsible for purchasing local health care services. This initiative was seen to be ground breaking because it demonstrated that all local GPs could be integrated into the corporate management arrangements of a health authority-based health care system. As such, it helped convince government to devise the national primary care group policy with its intention of involving all general practitioners in the corporate management of the NHS. However, in implementing the policy three paradoxes were present across chief executive 2's health system. First, in spite of the considerable local environmental instability the primary care groups were created satisfactorily, at least in terms of the configuration being led and agreed by local GPs and the chief executive. Second, local players accepted that the transition to primary care groups was a smooth process with no specific implementation problems. Third, despite chief executive 2's aforementioned historical ground-breaking activities with GPs, it was difficult to find positive comments from local players about the corporate management and leadership capability of the chief executive's executive team and organisation.

Although chief executive 2 was visible in leading change generally and was personally respected and trusted, his organisation was viewed as not having a strong executive team. The difficulties in forming effective interpersonally based networks were in evidence, and meant that the health authority struggled to construct longer-term, inter-organisational relationships sustainable enough to tackle difficult local challenges. The health authority had difficult relationships with its local trusts that in turn had difficult relationships with the emerging primary care groups, for example over improvements to, and expansion of, clinical services. Finally, there were difficult relationships between the health authority and the GP-led local medical committee, NHS headquarters and local government. The apparent lack of strength and depth of the relationship between the health authority and local government was exemplified by the latter's decision to commission its own strategic review of local health services, which resulted in the health authority being criticised for being too parochial in its strategic analysis of future health care service requirements for the local population.

In conclusion, neither the chief executive nor his executive team seemed able to practise effective networking or cross-boundary management by developing positive interpersonal and inter-organisational relationships. The chief executive gave the strong impression of reacting to local events and muddling through rather than being able to exercise leadership and positive influence over key players across the local health system. The research results paint a negative picture of an organisation that failed to:

- demonstrate leadership in terms of successfully concluding significant local issues such as future strategy for acute hospital services;
- find consensus and act decisively across the local health system because of the dominance of local players;
- work collaboratively by establishing networks with individuals and other organisations both NHS and non-NHS, even though the chief executive espoused partnership working.

Chief executive 3

Chief executive 3 led a semi-rural health system located in central England. In contrast to the three other case studies, general practitioner support for the primary care group policy flowed from the historic, ideological antipathy of local GPs to the former Conservative government's fundholding policy, in which individual GPs could hold budgets for purchasing local health services. Over time this stance had resulted in GP integration into the health authority's hierarchical management arrangements, which were much more bureaucratic and formal than in the three other health authorities. Project boards, service planning groups and GP forums all flourished as a result of chief executive 3's preferred approach to management and leadership.

In common with the approach across the rest of the English NHS, implementation of the primary care group policy by chief executive 3 involved consideration of a number of configuration options for establishing the groups. Also, in common with two of the other health authorities featured in this research, the former GP fundholders, who were small in number, also requested that they be allowed to form their own primary care group. The proposal was not granted, with the decision being supported by the overwhelming number of non-fundholding GPs, partly because some saw the proposal as being led by an idiosyncratic GP pursuing personal rather than corporate objectives. And in common with chief executive 1, chief executive 3 was also unsuccessful in securing national support for a variation to the national rules for establishing primary care groups.

The implementation issues experienced by chief executive 3 focused on local players' perceptions of control of the health care system being exercised by the chief executive and her executive team. Local players viewed chief executive 3's health authority as internally focused, centralised and controlling. They also viewed the organisation as failing, within a local environment of relative strategic stability, to exert sufficient influence on significant local issues, for example the strategic direction of certain clinical services and the organisational power of the large university hospital. This picture is in considerable contrast to chief executive 1 who made much more progress in formulating and agreeing local strategy and establishing effective inter-organisational networks. Chief executive 3 had two things in common with chief executive 2: although both were viewed positively by local players because of their integrity and commitment, their executive teams were not. As indicated above, chief executive 3 had historically managed the local health system by absorbing key local players, such as GPs and NHS Trusts, into the health authority's bureaucratic, committee-based management arrangements. The chief executive proposed to adopt the same approach to the primary care groups, which generated anxious questions from local players about the extent to which chief executive 3 was prepared to change her style and devolve power and responsibilities to the newly created primary care groups. Although local players could see a change of structure resulting from the emergence of the primary care groups they could not see a change of organisational culture.

The four health authorities and their chief executives were at a crossroads of major change because of the implications for the future management and leadership role of health authorities flowing from the introduction of primary care groups. It was clear that power and control had to be devolved to the new groups if they were to have any impact on improving health care services for their local populations. However, chief executive 3 differed from the other three chief executives because she had not yet made a demonstrable commitment to adapting her organisation's management arrangements to reflect the introduction of the groups. Although chief executive 3 implemented the national primary care group policy, this was against the backdrop of having had limited success in building a managerially strong local health system. Problems had been experienced over the development of a cardiac unit for the area and the local university hospital was viewed by most players as unacceptably dominant in inter-organisational relationships. Resistance to chief executive 3 and the relatively weak executive team was present throughout the health system, which adversely affected the health authority's ability to form strong interpersonal networks and sustainable longer-term inter-organisational relationships. This is in contrast to the personal and organisational success of chief executives 1 and 4, which flowed largely from network-based, interpersonal and inter-organisational relationships, and an effective and credibly viewed executive team.

Chief executive 3's actions in implementing the primary care policy were seen as a largely reactive and controlling approach to external events. Reflecting management rather than leadership, chief executive 3 continued to manage the local health system as a hierarchically driven, mainly internally focused organisation. She was concerned with maintaining stability, control and the status quo rather than with inspiring players with a vision for change. Further, in the light of the new primary care group policy, chief executive 3 showed no evidence of adapting to the new networks and relationships being generated as a result of what the management literature says is a continual shaping and re-shaping of the environment by the actions of external players, in this case local general practitioners.

Chief executive 4

Chief executive 4 led a large city-based health system in central England. The motivation for local general practitioners to support the primary care group policy was an extension of their general support for the GP commissioning policies of the previous government. What was different about chief executive

4's implementation of the primary care group policy is that he did not adopt the approach of the other three health authorities. He did not start with a predetermined view of the likely number and configuration of primary care groups across the health system. Although in common with all health authority chief executives, chief executive 4 was accountable to government for implementation of the primary care group, his approach was to agree that another powerful player, the GP-led local medical committee (LMC) should be seen to lead the process for determining the configuration of groups.

The reason for chief executive 4's approach was because he believed that the LMC would have a higher probability then he would of reaching agreement with local players, principally GPs, on the configuration of groups. The chief executive had a clear understanding of the local context and interpersonal and inter-organisational networks, and his assessment was that in contrast to the health authority, the local medical committee had a longer history of trusting relationships with GPs. There was also a strong and trusting relationship between the health authority and local medical committee, which was also why the chief executive adopted the approach he did. This relationship between the two organisations was the only example from the four case studies of networking developing into inter-organisational collaboration (see Table 4.1 on page 84). Chief executive 4's health system was moving from a highly fragmented environment of GP commissioning groups, unique among the four health authorities, to implementing the unified system of primary care groups. The risk for the chief executive directly flowed from the decision to pursue implementation of the primary care group policy through the local medical committee, a third-party trade union-based organisation responsible for representing the professional interests of general practitioners, which is not formally part of the NHS hierarchy. It is also important to note that since general practitioners contract independently with the NHS (they are not directly employed) neither the health authority nor the local medical committee were able to exert direct managerial control over them. They had to work on the basis of interpersonal influence.

Chief executive 4's two implementation issues involved disagreements over the configuration of the primary care groups. They were however different in tone from those experienced elsewhere because they focused on election irregularities of the chair to one of the groups; and considerable political and legal involvement precipitated by a request from some GPs to form their own primary care group. Both these issues were eventually resolved satisfactorily. The views of external players of chief executive 4 and his executive team were generally positive, and players commented on their strategic development work with its strong externally focused, inclusive and listening style. In many ways this compared to chief executive 2's approach to strategy formulation but in complete contrast to chief executive 2, chief executive 4 had stronger inter-personal and inter-organisational networks that were more influential and effective in helping to shape a new future. In common with chief executive 1, chief executive 4 was more decisive and pragmatic. For example, he also had taken an iterative approach to the formulation of local strategy. He initi-ated an external review of the formulation of strategy for local acute hospital services thus demonstrating a willingness to listen and learn from the views of others. This was in contrast to chief executive 2's internally driven approach to formulating strategy, which was frequently challenged.

Reflecting on leadership visibility, chief executives 2 and 3 were personally seen to have taken a high-profile, leading role during the implementation of the primary care group policy although their largely managerial approach was unlikely to result in strong and sustainable interpersonal and inter-organisational relationships in the longer term. In contrast, for the reasons outlined above, neither chief executive 1 nor chief executive 4 were particularly visible during the implementation of the primary care group policy. However, the strength of their executive teams, coupled with well-developed interpersonal networks comprising local leaders meant that the lack of chief executive visibility did not adversely affect the sustainability of inter-organisational relationships between the health authorities and key external players. They did however, demonstrate visibility when it was required, for example when implementation difficulties arose. In summary, in common with chief executive 1, chief executive 4 had exercised leadership and created an externally focused network-based organisa-tion. Both factors were important to chief executive 4's personal and organisa-tional success in terms of achieving a successful balance between implement-ing externally driven national change, such as the primary care group policy and tackling important local issues, such as the formulation of strategy for acute hospital services.

Conclusion

Both chief executive 1 and chief executive 4 made considerable progress in determining longer-term strategy for their acute hospital services, albeit in different ways in terms of process. In contrast, chief executive 2 had been strug-gling to conclude the same single, big strategic issue for many years at the same time as trying to establish financial control across the local health system. The research results for chief executive 2 show these issues dominating inter-organisational relationships and this was the most striking example of relationship difficulties in the four case studies. Turning to chief executive 3, the health system appeared to be stable but significant contextual issues included the dominance of the university hospital and the decision-making process for establishing a new cardiac unit. In common with the strategic and financial issues that faced the three other chief executives, chief executive 3's contextual issues pre-dated the election of the 1997 Labour government. Although chief executive 1 achieved a conclusion to the strategic review of acute hospital services, his actions resulted in the temporary breakdown of relationships with local general practitioners. Chief executive 2, who attempted to agree a similar local strategy at about the same time as chief executive 1, continued to experience uncertainty and inter-organisational friction and did not reach a conclusion. Chief executive 3 did secure agreement to create a local cardiac surgery unit but the eventual location was not the result of the health authority's proactive planning and leadership but the opportunistic actions of a local NHS Trust working through its own effective networks with key clinical staff.

The case studies clearly show that health care chief executives have local as well as national objectives indicating that contextual demands flow from both national and local requirements and pressures. The former comprises mainly nationally driven policies and structural change programmes; while the latter revolves around complex and often politically challenging local challenges such as strategy determination, financial control and the development of local services. What the experience of the four chief executives shows is that how they responded to the changes was largely left to local discretion. It was not national government that drove chief executives 1, 2 and 4 to decide to pursue strategies to rationalise their acute hospital services and chief executive 3 to pursue the smaller, but equally important, strategy for creating a local cardiac surgery unit. These were local decisions arising from discussions about health needs, the future of clinical services and the influence of clinical professionals. The experience of the four chief executives shows that both process and consequences could be difficult to manage in terms of securing wide-ranging support for change, decision-making and implementation. The decision of the four chief executives to pursue these significant local challenges reflects the management literature in that although constraints on senior managerial jobs in health care can be considerable the demand element of the job is actually small. In other words, health care leaders can choose to not only tackle as many or as few significant local issues as they wish but also the timescale within which they are addressed. This is an important point in understanding the leadership role of health care chief executives, which is insufficiently acknowledged in public sector management research.

In summary, it is the aims and objectives of the four chief executives and their organisations, interacting with their local operating environment that primarily drives the tackling of important local issues. And the research presented here shows that the process of how these issues are tackled does influence the views of local players about the overall leadership of the local health system undertaken by chief executives and their executive teams. An important question is, are the differing local contexts for the four chief executives relevant when implementing nationally driven change? Perhaps the answer is 'no' because the four chief executives complied fully with the content and timescale of the government's policy to create primary care groups 16 months after its announcement. What is clear from the research results is that the inter-organisational history of the health systems, coupled with how the chief executives tackled local issues, drove the different approaches to implementation of nationally driven policy. Specifically, the research results show each chief executive taking into account their respective histories of local strategy formulation, the history of general practitioner involvement in the corporate management of the local health care system, and the strengths and weaknesses of interpersonal and inter-organisational relationships. It is these histories, generated largely from the historical tackling of significant local issues, with the resultant impact on interpersonal and inter-organisational health authority relationships with key players, that are important when determining the process for implementing nationally driven change, such as that associated with government policy. Consequently, the first research proposition is supported, namely that the operating environment or context is different and its successful management is important to personal and organisational success for health care system leaders.

The second research proposition is that health authorities have become externally focused network-based organisations and this too is important to personal and organisational success for health system leaders. However, the proposition is only partly supported by the research results. Only chief executive 1 and chief executive 4 developed a leadership style and culture and although chief executive 2 and chief executive 3 implemented the national primary care group policy they had limited success in tackling significant local challenges. The success of chief executive 1 and chief executive 4 flowed in part from their development of a network-based approach to tackling local and nationally driven health system-wide change. That involved the chief executives developing effective interpersonal and inter-organisational relationships with key local players such as general practitioners, their professional representative bodies and local government authorities. Chief executive 1 and chief executive 4 also demonstrated a successful balance between achieving nationally and locally driven objectives, which in turn provided greater strategic, financial and overall inter-organisational stability across their local health systems.

In contrast, chief executives 2 and 3 experienced considerable difficulties in agreeing local strategy, achieving financial control and establishing effective inter-organisational networks. They seemed unable to create the necessary degree of local stability as the basis for implementing nationally driven change. The difficulty for these two chief executives in creating a leadership culture was for three interrelated reasons:

- first, an inability to develop an effective and respected executive team as viewed by local players;
- second, an inability to develop effective and sustainable interpersonal and inter-organisational relationships;
- third, an inability to develop and work with other leaders across the local health care system by, among other things, sharing power and decision-making.

Finally, a paradox was evident from the actions of chief executive 1 and chief executive 4: the relative inter-organisational stability and interpersonal trust that emerged from the successful tackling of significant local challenges created a strong basis for the successful implementation of further, externally, nationally driven change. In this context, paradox would be defined as something that is surprising or an observation that counters common beliefs. In other words, it is counter-intuitive to think that stability can arise from deliberately pursuing big change. In many ways, chief executive 1's leadership style was paradoxical in that he clearly led but kept himself in the background. The main advantage of thinking about paradox is its value in making sense of the context within which we work and pursue change. Focusing on the paradoxes of daily managerial life may not be particularly satisfying but it probably paints a more realistic and recognisable picture for practising managers and leaders than the theoretical linear view of the world of complex management and change that is often presented. In conclusion, it can be seen from the analysis of the four case studies that the third research proposition is supported, namely that health care system leadership is rooted in achieving a balance between implementing nationally driven policy (such as that from government) and achieving locally significant driven objectives, which taken together constitutes overall personal and organisational success for health care system leaders.

A MODEL FOR HEALTH CARE LEADERSHIP

These research results show that leadership is not required to successfully implement major or nationally driven change such as that arising from government policy. A managerial or transactional approach is sufficient for governmental needs. However, the case studies show that a managerial approach is unlikely to produce longer-term sustainable change whether implementing nationally driven change or tackling significant, local strategic change. What the research does show is that it is possible for health care leaders to successfully develop a leadership style and culture based on the following threefold approach:

1   aligning the cultural, relationship and decision-making history of the local health care system with the challenges of the present in order to achieve success in the future;

2   the successful tackling of significant local challenges such as determining the strategic direction for services and achieving financial stability;

3   pursuing an approach based on developing effective interpersonal based networking and inter-organisational relationships supported by a competent and externally respected executive team.

The research shows that the above variables are critical to chief executive personal and organisational success and the overall approach presented here is most likely to shape and drive successful and sustainable implementation of change whether locally or nationally driven. The results have been translated into a model for health care chief executive leadership (Goodwin ibid.). The model (see Figure 6.1) shows that the extent to which chief executive leadership effectiveness can be developed is determined by the interaction between national and local objectives and the behaviour of the chief executive in terms of being influenced by, or influencing, the five interconnected variables in the inner circle. The interconnected variables are:

1   the quality of the chief executive's executive team, as perceived by external players;

2   the history of local inter-organisational relationships in terms of understanding how they were formed and who are seen to be the leaders and individuals of influence in these relationships;

3   the ability of the chief executive and executive team to establish sustainable interpersonal networks both within and across health care organisational boundaries;

4   the ability to build on networks and networking by developing inter-organisational alliances and partnerships, again both within and beyond the health care organisation's boundaries;

5   from the creation of alliances and partnerships, the extent to which the chief executive and executive team can share power and decision-making with other health care and non-health care organisations.

Figure 6.1 *Model for health care leadership*

CONCLUSION

The conclusions of this research take forward previous public sector management research. The research supports the conclusions of previous attitudinal-based research in terms of the views of the constraining environment for leaders of health care organisations operating in a political system. However, a paradox is evident because in spite of the apparent constraints it is still possible for health care leaders to practise leadership locally. This has not been demonstrated in any previous public sector management research and has important implications for the way that previous research is evaluated. Although management and leadership are not mutually exclusive there are differences. Management is essentially about stability and maintaining the status quo, while leadership is concerned with change and the future. What is clear however is that management is more formal or rational than leadership, intending to be used in generally similar ways across a wide range of situations. Therefore, limited leadership coupled with strong management could be appropriate at times of general stability, but at times of major or fast moving change, strong leadership coupled with limited management is more likely to be required.

The above definitions of management and leadership are taken from the review of the literature summarised in Chapter 1. In the context of this research and the above definition of leadership, change did take place in each health authority if only because they implemented the government's primary care group policy. However, purely because leadership and change may be correlated in some way, coupled with the chief executives implementing a national NHS change programme, the case studies show that chief executive leadership is not automatically found in each of the four health authorities. If management is about authority related to organisational position then leadership is about personal vision, influence and risk. Leaders of professionally based health care organisations are required to pursue organisational and inter-organisational agendas with little if any direct managerial control over external players such as clinical staff and external stakeholders such as local politicians. Therefore, to exercise influence, take risks and subsequently make decisions necessitates working through networks and relationships that connect these different individuals and organisations.

The four case studies presented in this chapter have summarised how real leaders of health care systems have tackled major challenges arising from locally and nationally driven pressure for change. Although the case study research focused on chief executives in England, the research results are as relevant to leaders at all levels in health care organisations and networks across Europe such as clinical directors and heads of services. In the complex, multi-organisational environment of European health care no leader can pursue leadership without the support of an able team and the creation of sustainable networks of other leaders and followers both within their organisation or service and across health care organisational boundaries.

DISCUSSION QUESTIONS

1   Do you understand the reasons for the success of two of the four chief executives presented in the research results? And conversely, do you understand why the other two chief executives were less successful?

2   This chapter was written to help to bridge the gap between the academic leadership literature and the real life practicalities of pursuing leadership. Does the research presented here help you to do that and can you see the links between the literature and practical leadership?

3   Can you think of examples of leadership successes and failures in your own
    health system and reflect on why that was, in the context of the findings of the
    research presented above? If so, on reflection would there be aspects of those
    leadership experiences that you consider should have been undertaken
    differently?

4   What do you consider to be the main lessons from this chapter for the
    personal leadership development of yourself and your team?

BIBLIOGRAPHY AND FURTHER READING

Bresnen M.J. (1995) All things to all people? Perceptions, attributions, and construc-
    tions of leadership. *Leadership Quarterly* 6(4): 495–513.

Bryman A. (1989) *Research Methods and Organization Studies*. London: Routledge.

Department of Health (1997) *The New NHS. Modern. Dependable*. London: HMSO.

Department of Health (2000) *The NHS. A plan for investment, a plan for reform*.
    London: HMSO.

Department of Health (2004) *The NHS Improvement Plan. Putting people at the
    heart of public services*. London: HMSO.

Goodwin N. (2002) *The Leadership Role of Chief Executives in the English NHS*.
    Unpublished PhD thesis. Manchester Business School, University of Manchester.

Hakim C. (1987) *Research Design. Strategies and choices in the design of social
    research*. London: Routledge.

Kumar R. (1999) *Research Methodology: A step-by-step guide for beginners*.
    London: Sage Publications Ltd.

Mitchell J.C. (1983) Case and situational analysis. *Sociological Review* 31:
    187–211.

Smircich L. and Morgan G. (1982) Leadership: the management of meaning. *The
    Journal of Applied Behavioral Science* 18(3): 257–273.

Chapter 7

Failing and learning

KEY TERMS

- Failure
- Mentoring
- Coaching
- Emotional intelligence
- Adversity
- Reflection and self-awareness
- Personal development
- Alpha males

INTRODUCTION

The previous chapters have shown that leadership is an interpersonal, dynamic relationship-based process. As such it is subject to the human foibles that we all possess. At one extreme however, leadership can be dangerous because the personal and interpersonal stresses from pursuing change can be great. Leadership demands respect for people's basic need for direction, protection and order and it requires compassion and support at times when change is distressing. This is often difficult to fulfil and consequently, leaders are always failing somebody and sometimes they fail themselves. Knowing how hard to push ourselves and others, when to pause and when to stop are important judgements to make as a leader. In pursuing leadership, people can be drawn to taking courageous stands, which in the worst excesses can result in personal career sacrifice and failure. This may be tempting to some because it promises ongoing permanence for the leader's words and actions. The illusion of career immortality can be a powerful and attractive action for leaders with grand ambitions or when facing great resistance to change. In short, emotions can be very powerful, which is why we discussed emotional intelligence in Chapter 5.

The aim of leadership development should be the development of long-term, sustainable, effective personal skills of individuals and teams. However, attending formal training courses away from the workplace is unlikely to result in long-term benefit because only a fraction of new knowledge is used and retained. This is because when leaders return to their work, the realities of their day-to-day lives and pressures, coupled with an associated lack of personal time, results in the learning not being thought through in the local context and subsequently applied. Consequently, organisations need to place greater emphasis on experiential learning in order to facilitate sustained personal behavioural and practice changes. A major qualitative and quantitative one-year longitudinal study of 50 R&D teams, comprising 50 leaders and over 300 team members, found evidence that leaders who learn from current and recent experience had a positive effect on their team's processes and performance (Hirst *et al.* 2004). Further, work-based learning, rather than off-site classroom learning, has a sustained impact on leadership behaviour, particularly so for new leaders. This approach is supported by the leadership development implications of Goodwin's (2002) research that correlates personal leadership success for health care chief executives with the successful management of significant change within their local contexts. Consequently, leadership development should be rooted in learning how to manage important local issues in the context of providing a national public service. Further, Alimo-Metcalfe and Lawler (2001) point out that analysis of how to develop future leaders cannot be undertaken separate from understanding how chief executives and others who are perceived to be leaders exert influence.

But why discuss failure, and why is it important to personal leadership development? There are links between leadership failure and self-esteem and emotional intelligence. It is no surprise that self-esteem increases with success and decreases temporarily at times of failure. However, good leaders are unlikely to be emotionally destabilised when failure occurs: and the very best leaders are those with a fine-tuned intuition to which they listen. These people have an ability to understand not only their own feelings but the feelings of others without words, to grasp what others value and so are able to get the best out of people. Such skills are rare however, the more so in men. Women tend to be much more attuned to their feelings and those of others than their male counterparts. Intuition and feelings are important personal characteristics at times of failure because if failed leaders are wise and have developed their self-awareness, they will look dispassionately at what went wrong and extract the learning when in similar circumstances in the future.

Placing personal learning from failure into the wider context of developing yourself and your team starts with understanding and managing yourself. To do that you need to have self-awareness and self-confidence in your ability to cope in your job, recognise when you need personal support from a colleague, mentor or coach, or to ask a team member to take over the leadership of a specific issue on your behalf. To achieve that necessitates understanding your strengths and weaknesses in terms of personal skills, experience and know-ledge. This starts with understanding how you work because it would be unusual for us to devote equal amounts of time and energy to all components of our jobs. There are parts of our job that we enjoy and concentrate on more than others, resulting in other parts that we are likely to devote too little attention to or possibly ignore altogether. This is all part of having sufficient self-awareness of the need to learn about ourselves and the job that we do, including those situations and aspects of the job likely to produce symptoms of stress.

FAILURE

It is important to explore failure because it is a feature of most aspects of our lives as we grow and personally develop. Learning to personally cope with failure and manage its consequences is a key attribute of successful leaders. Failures can be big or small, and some are discovered while others remain hidden. Some leaders, principally chief executives and senior clinical staff, may face public dismissal because of their failures, while others are never held to account for their actions perhaps because their failure remains undiscovered or is never made public for organisational, political or some other reason. If nothing else, this reminds us that life is inherently unfair. Failure is insidious. There are times when failure occurs because of a single incident but more often than not it builds up over time; and sometimes it occurs without anyone spotting how it started or being able to stop it. In health care organisations failure can occur in a number of areas: strategy implementation, operational or financial management, clinical practice and system failure. The most visible failures are the ones at the top involving board directors and senior clinical staff but less high-profile failures will often include middle managers and junior clinical staff. In addition to learning from failure, another reason for discussing it is because there is so much of it. We live and work in demanding times and the health care environment is more complex than ever before. Even the most talented leader will struggle from time to time and occasionally fail.

We have seen from the public sector management literature in Chapter 3 that lessons from the private sector cannot be translated easily to the public sector because of fundamental differences in the way public services are organised and led, their relationship to government and politics, competing professional interests, and the difficulty in formulating and measuring objectives. Consequently, issues raised in the private sector need to be understood and translated cautiously into a public sector context. There are no generally accepted definitions of what constitutes organisational failure and it is a subjective and often contested term (Walsh et al. 2004). Commercial organisations will use quantitative measures to track performance such as return on investment or trends in profitability. But the point at which poor performance becomes failure can be difficult to define and may be determined internally by senior management or externally by company shareholders or the financial institutions supporting the commercial enterprise. There is of course nothing particularly superior about private companies and their handling of failure. Although all organisations are susceptible to error and failure the difference between public and private organisations is that historically, the approach to correcting failure in the private sector operates either weakly or not at all in public services. In public services, failure focuses on the meeting of statutory or governmental responsibilities to the public, the effective management of resources to reach those in need, the provision of safe, consistent and reliable services, and the requirement to provide efficient, economic and effective services. However, there are significant differences when comparing failure in health care organisations with failure in a commercial organisation (Walshe and Shortell 2004). In the private sector, failure is linked largely to economic measures such as market share, financial viability, profitability, and ultimately, company survival. A major service failure in a production-based company for example, is likely to close or slow down production with resultant costs to the organisation and its staff. If the failure is significant, perhaps as the result of an industrial accident or incident, and has caused casualties then some staff are likely to be among those injured. It is not surprising therefore that private sector companies have developed strong cultures and systems for failure awareness. In contrast, it is often normal for health care organisations to carry on with their work even after the most serious failure and it is patients rather than staff who bear almost the entire cost of the failure.

In health care, many organisations face multi-factorial failure reflecting poor leadership in areas such as clinical, financial and performance management and governance. Walshe and Shortell (ibid.) have researched examples of major health care service failures from six countries (the United States, the United Kingdom, Australia, New Zealand, Canada and the Netherlands) to explore how health care systems and organisations deal with these failures. They defined major failure as breakdowns in health care services or provision that do substantial harm to many patients. The culture of health care organisations is because not everyone can be treated or cared for successfully then it is acceptable for patients to die. Consequently, when things do go wrong it can be difficult for health care organisations and their leaders to develop corporate self-awareness so that they are able to view the failure and the reasons for it objectively. For example, a public inquiry into paediatric cardiac surgery at the Bristol Royal Infirmary in England concluded that about 35 patient deaths were potentially avoidable if cardiac surgeons had not ignored repeated warnings about poor surgical quality outcomes and continued to operate on newborn children (HMG 2001).

We have seen from Chapter 3 that international, national and local contexts for health and health care can be complex and fast moving. For European health care leaders this is likely to be the case for some time to come because of consumer pressure and an increasing emphasis in most countries on the reform of health care systems. Consequently, understanding context is not always easy and sometimes even talented leaders are destined to fail because of that. The previous chapter about the four health care chief executives has shown that there are numerous reasons why leaders fail, which are often related to their personal style and approach to the leadership process:

- Leaders struggle to implement their visions for change. They fail because they cannot achieve their organisational or team objectives, they appear to be indecisive and they do not deliver on personal commitments. Sometimes this is because the leader will use the same process for each occasion, failing to learn from past events and trying new situations.
- Some leaders have an over preoccupation with strategy and vision because of the mistaken belief that taking time to develop exactly the right strategy or vision is the sole route to organisational success. As the previous chapters have shown, there is not a single approach to successful leadership.
- Leaders cannot deal with people. They fail here because they do not put the right people in the right jobs including those in their own teams. The leader also fails to establish effective interpersonal relationships with people in the team's wider networks. Finally, the leader fails to resolve people problems sufficiently quickly, which are rarely unobserved by wider stakeholders as the story of the four chief executives in Chapter 6 showed.
- Leaders become too focused on process to the detriment of outcome. Consequently, meetings become time-consuming formalities, cordiality and facilitation take over from constructive and challenging debate. The result of an over emphasis on process is that creativity and the development of sustainable networks for change becomes lost. This is linked to the first point because an over preoccupation with process can be linked to indecision as some of the chief executives in the previous chapter exemplified.

The diagnosis or acknowledgement of organisational failure is usually preceded by a period of declining performance. An absence of leadership is one factor in high-profile organisational tragedies (Higgins 2001; Øvretveit 2004) while major failures in health care are a product of the distinctive culture of health care organisations and their professional staff whether across Europe or internationally (Walshe and Shortell ibid.). This is because professionally based organisations can generate endemic secrecy, deference to authority, defensiveness and professional protectionism, interests that are too often subordinated to the corporate interests of health care organisations, their staff and consumers. Since the UK NHS was formed in 1948 over 30 public inquiries have been conducted to address significant failures in the quality of care provided to patients by numerous organisations. In addition to the absence of leadership, there are four other significant themes emerging for the reasons for the failures occurring (Higgins ibid.):

■ organisational or service isolation, which leaves clinical staff and others left behind by organisational and service developments elsewhere and unaware of new ideas or, alternatively, suspicious of them;

■ failure of systems and processes because either they are not present or not working properly;

■ poor communication both within the health care organisation and between it and its staff and consumers;

■ a disempowerment of staff and consumers so that those who might have raised concerns about services or organisational or service leadership issues were discouraged from doing so.

It can be normal for the acceptance of failure to be delayed by internal or external stakeholders because they do not see the problem, or they perhaps ignore it or even cover it up. When failure is eventually acknowledged it rarely comes as a surprise. For some, the acknowledgement may even be a relief or viewed positively because it will force the need for action. In the light of the above findings there are probably three phases in the decline and fall of leaders of organisations or services:

1   Initially, the leader will begin to lose his or her grasp on reality. This will often follow a period of sustained success for the leader, which for some can generate overconfidence and arrogance. There are links here with the concept of bad leadership discussed in Chapter 1 (Kellerman 2004). The result is often a lack of objectivity in assessing the achievability and risks of future leadership proposals. The risk of failure increases from this stage onwards.

2   The second stage, following the arrogance and lack of self-awareness of the first stage, is the leader's increasing insensitivity to the contribution and feelings of those around them. The leader will stop listening to their team and other close colleagues. Instead, he or she increasingly will see their own version of reality and consequently believe in their own version of the truth. The leader will resist attempts by others to present an alternative reality and eventually close colleagues will become demotivated and stop

offering support and constructive criticism. At this stage errors will begin to occur.

3   The final stage is complete loss of faith in the leader. Other key players within the organisation, along with external stakeholders, begin to believe instead the evidence of the leader's team. The risk of significant failure is high, as stakeholders will often observe dysfunctional leadership. At this stage there is little choice but to replace the leader.

LEARNING FROM FAILURE

How do people cope with difficult situations and also learn from them? We have seen from previous chapters that successful leaders need to be both active and reflective. They need to deliver results for their followers, for their organisations or services and for themselves. Leaders also need to have the necessary self-awareness skills to review past leadership experiences for personal growth and development. Having said that, for a leader to alternate between participating in events and observing both themselves and those around them can be difficult. The risk is that rather than maintaining perspective on surrounding events, leaders can often become swept up by them resulting in a loss of perspective and the risk of failure. But why is it that certain people seem to naturally inspire confidence, loyalty and hard work while others stumble, again and again? There is no simple answer but Bennis and Thomas (2002) believe it has something to do with the different ways that people deal with adversity. They say that one of the most reliable indicators and predictors of true leadership is an individual's ability to find meaning in negative events and to learn from even the most trying circumstances. In other words, the personal skills required to successfully address adversity and emerge stronger and more committed are the same ones that make for extraordinary leaders.

The importance of adversity is also reflected in Heifitz's (2003) development of adaptive capacity, which he describes as the ability to transcend adversity with all its associated stresses and to emerge stronger than before. It comprises two primary qualities: the ability to grasp context, and hardiness. The former is about the ability to assess a number of variables, ranging from how many different groups of people will interpret a policy or organisational or personal gesture to being able to put a situation in perspective. Without this leaders are utterly lost because they cannot connect with their followers. Hardiness is perseverance and toughness, which enables people to emerge from difficult circumstances or failure without losing hope. It is the combination of hardiness and ability to grasp context that above all, allows a person not only to survive an ordeal but to learn from it and to emerge stronger and more committed than before.

The real question for leaders is not whether they fail but how they handle it when they do. For some people, failure is a spur. Those leaders who have suffered or overcome hurdles in their early life – such as loss of a parent or poor educational attainment – have often developed ways for dealing with adversity, which stands them in good stead when hit by a personal or professional failure in later life. The more successful leaders tend to bounce back from adversity within a few days accepting they may have made a poor decision and using it as a learning experience. Experienced, practising managers and leaders know that in organisational life decisions are rarely, if ever, wholly right. Rather, decisions tend be made on a spectrum between good and poor. Consequently, it is equally rare for decisions to be wholly wrong, except of course when bad leaders make decisions.

In an extensive review of the literature on turning around failing organisations, leadership, strategy, openness to learning and the involvement of staff all emerge as important to success (Barnes 2003). Turning to public service organisations, in an examination of leadership behaviour during a successful turnaround of a UK local (municipal) authority in the late 1990s, Joyce (2004) reached a number of important conclusions about the role of leadership in that context. Although leaders are rightly concerned with developing and communicating a vision of the future they are equally likely to be interested in acquiring a detailed knowledge not only of performance but also the local context and politics in which the organisation's activities take place. Consequently, the leader will not only be highly visible but also involved in detailed management issues as well as the big picture aspects of leadership. In turnaround situations the leader will have to pursue not only empowering staff but also leading them into uncomfortable territory in order, among other things, to encourage them to become accountable for future personal and organisational performance. For the leader, this is likely to present the challenge of ensuring that he or she has sufficient personal resilience to lead the necessary changes. In addition, in organisations with a strong political influence such as health care, managerial leaders will only be successful in pursuing their vision of the future if they are supported by the aspirations of politicians.

The implication of the above research, in common with the chief executive-based research results presented in Chapter 6 (Goodwin 2002), is that effective leaders also manage the detail. What this means is that for leaders to be successful they have to do more than simply articulate visions and values that reflect the shared aspirations of staff and external stakeholders such as professional groups and politicians. These leaders understand the detail of implementing change; have a detailed knowledge of the business of their organisation or service; and they ensure that operational objectives are tackled in a timely and effective way. They also address resistance to change and conflict, which importantly is a characteristic not wholly addressed in the theory of transformational leadership (Joyce ibid.). The work of Glanfield *et al.* (2004), based on poorly performing health care organisations, has led to the development of a qualitative framework to review, assess, plan and intervene at operational and strategic levels in order to help determine what is going well and not well within an organisation. The five components of the framework, which reflects much of the content of this and previous chapters, are as follows:

1 Leadership and direction

This is seen as important because the extent to which people have confidence and trust in their own leadership and the leadership of others is crucial. Kanter (2004) argues that self-confidence is not the real secret of leadership but the confidence the leader has in other people. This is because leadership involves motivating others to achieve their finest efforts and leaders must believe that for organisational and personal success, they can count on other people to deliver. When people have confidence in one another they are willing not only to lead but also to be led.

2 Quantity and quality of connections

This is about relationships. Chapter 6 on the four chief executives has shown that relationship building is crucial to personal and organisational leadership success. Consequently, in some places it is possible to get things done because there are good quality, trusting relationships while elsewhere that is not the case. In the case of organisations or network-based services spread across multiple sites there is an increased risk of geographical isolation, particularly between staff and senior management and with stakeholders of other organisations. This generates greater leadership pressure because additional leadership effort, in terms of time and communications, will be required in such circumstances.

3 Power and authority

Leadership cannot be discussed without incorporating power and authority. The exercise of power is necessary to bring about change, and for change to be sustainable there must be an appropriate distribution of power within any given context. People can become more effective by working with and through other people; and by relinquishing some power in order for others to take more control over their own work and service. As Chapter 4 on networks showed, the sharing of power, sometimes between different organisations, is important if successful partnership and collaboration is to be secured.

4 Inclusion and contribution

This is important because as the literature presented above implies, there are many stories about failure in which people knew what was going wrong but they were ignored when they tried to raise concerns. Consequently, it is important not only to maintain networks and formal and informal dialogue to know what is going on, but, equally importantly, to know where to go to find out what is going on. This is about using networks and 'soft' information. Chapter 4 on networks and partnerships referred to 'soft' information playing a valuable role in complementing the use of 'hard' information to performance-assess health care organisations (Goddard *et al.* 1999).

5 Control of core business

Core business is the principle reason for an organisation or network's existence, whether public or private. Consequently, the successful delivery and achievement of core objectives is crucial for all organisations, not only for organisational survival but also because it provides stability and freedom to develop wider business objectives. The control of core business explores the leadership aspect of the extent to which systems and processes either enable or prevent people from working effectively, evaluating their performance and taking corrective action if necessary.

Failure is a normal part of development for everyone, whether working in the private or public sector, and whether new or experienced leader. History shows that some of the greatest successes emerge from failure and perseverance. For all leaders, at whatever level, the approach to coping with and moving beyond failure is about perspective, analysis and learning. Consequently, we need to:

- Put the failure into perspective, trying not to personalise it and to get over it as soon as possible. Difficult though this is at the time the failure occurs, we should try to move forward and not to dwell on what has happened.
- Analyse the failure, studying what has gone wrong and why. In doing this we need to be objective, and discussing the failure with a trusted colleague, mentor or coach can help achieve that.

■   Learn from the failure, which is the most important reason for reflecting on it. We need to understand that above all else, failure teaches us what not to do and that if faced with the same or similar situation again we need to respond and behave differently.

We all experience disappointment and failure throughout our lives. But we will be wiser and develop more effectively if we can reconcile ourselves to failure in our careers just as we have to in our personal lives. Consequently, the most important and only significant reason for discussing and analysing failure is to learn from it. Experiencing failure, coupled with a willingness to learn from it, is a good reason for taking responsibility for our own personal learning and development. To learn from failure requires a process of personal reflection, which cannot be taught in a classroom. In his book *Managers not MBAs*, Mintzberg (2004) argues for a wholly different approach to developing managers. He says that many management programmes promise a 'boot camp' approach, meaning that although participants are worked hard, this provides little opportunity to stop and think. Managers need to step back from their day-to-day lives and reflect thoughtfully on their managerial and leadership experiences. In other words, personal learning is not doing – it is reflecting on doing. It is important however to note that according to Mintzberg reflecting does not mean gazing into space and musing inside one's head. It is far from being a casual process. What reflecting means is wondering, probing, analysing, synthesizing, and connecting to one's inner-self. It is necessary to think not just about what has happened but why it has happened and how the situation under reflection is similar and different from other issues. Equally importantly, when reflecting on our roles and actions in situations we should reflect first and foremost on our strengths because this is the most important thing for the successful executive to know about himself or herself (Drucker 2005). The process is enhanced if 360° or other feedback analysis is used. Alternatively, adopt the practice of Drucker himself by writing down what you expect to happen whenever you make a key decision and some months later compare the actual results with your expectations. This then would form the basis of your reflection including determining whether your strengths were used to produce the best results. In the light of the reflection could your strengths be improved or did any bad habits or lack of knowledge emerge that inhibited your personal effectiveness?

Mintzberg (ibid.) argues for a process of 'experienced reflection'. This involves managers bringing their experience to the classroom, where the faculty introduce various concepts, theories and models. Although all reflection is primarily personal, managers can also reflect together in discussion. Managers live in the territory of their own experience while academic faculty provide the maps. Reflection takes place where these meet: experience considered in the light of conceptual ideas. The resultant learning is carried back to the place of work, where it impacts on behaviour, thereby providing further experience for reflection at work to bring back to the classroom. In short, this constitutes a recurring cycle from work experience to reflection and learning in the classroom and then back to the workplace, and so on. The point about experienced reflection is that it confronts new ideas with established beliefs both individually and in discussion with other managers. Approaches to personal development proposed by Mintzberg are probably rare and the more traditional lecture and case study analytical methods will be the norm in many academic institutions. These approaches are not discussed here and information about them is readily available from relevant academic institutions and personnel/human resources departments within employing organisations. What is now discussed, in the light of the comments about the need for reflection in pursuing personal development, is mentoring and coaching. This is because these are discursive and reflective-based approaches to career development, within which failure can be explored for personal learning.

MENTORING AND COACHING

Mentoring

It is often remarkable how many clever, highly motivated and responsible people rarely pause to contemplate their own behaviour. Many people are often more inclined to move on than to reflect on past performance and many will reach the top without addressing their limitations. The objective of coaching and mentoring is to help and support individuals to manage their personal learning in order for them to maximise their potential, to develop their skills and improve their performance (Parslowe and Wray 2003). The terms coaching and mentoring are used to describe a wide variety of activities but there are distinctions. Mentors will often seek to develop a special relationship as close as possible to the traditional concept of a trusted adviser and counsellor and the mentor will rarely be the mentee's line manager. Coaching tends to be an enabling and helping process while mentoring is essentially a supportive process. Coaches and mentors have to be teachers because of their responsibilities to develop their own staff and assist colleagues by sharing ideas and experiences.

In general, both the mentor and the mentee are likely to be more interested in improvements in the latter's performance and behaviour over a longer timescale than is the case with coaching. Mentoring helps to progress individual careers by increasing personal self-esteem and satisfaction and helping individuals use their intelligence more fully to make a contribution to personal and organisational success. The process of mentoring tends to be paternalistic in that it provides a role model for the individual to follow. Mentors will use their greater knowledge, experience and status to help the individual and generally will do more than merely act supportively or give advice. For example, mentors may assist in enhancing the mentee's visibility and advancement within the organisation or across business networks by speaking supportively of them, or by the mentor allowing the mentee to shadow them at meetings and other events. In their review of the literature on gender and race in mentoring relationships Clutterbuck and Ragins (2002) conclude that some but not all research has suggested that women, and people from black and minority ethnic backgrounds receive different amounts and types of mentoring functions than white males. Although male and female mentors provide the same types of mentoring functions, mentor gender affects outcomes. Also, mentees often find it difficult to set personal development goals; for example, help is likely to be required in defining less-tangible goals such as building self-confidence. A contributory factor may be a relatively low level of self-awareness, but whether that is the result of low motivation to explore the inner self; or low motivation to avoid such exploration, or simply an inability to make complex emotional and rational connections, is unclear.

Coaching

Coaching refers to training, that is guidance and feedback about specific efforts involved in a task, the performance of a job, and the handling of assignments. The broad field of coaching includes life planning, career counselling, health advice and training in specific skills. There has been increasing interest in coaching, which may be the result of this more holistic, societal approach being taken by people in general and the business world in particular. The development of professional coaching in business can be traced to the USA in the 1980s (Hudson 1999) with an acceleration taking place precipitated by the need for human caring during the period of downsizing, mergers, acquisitions and outplacements in corporate America. Almost inevitably, the US growth in demand for coaching in the business world transferred to the UK, and to a lesser extent Europe. However, by 2002 the European Mentoring and Coaching Council had been established, which aims to promote good practice and the expectation of good practice in mentoring and coaching, and to ensure that the best possible standards are maintained. The research on the contribution that coaching can make to executive development is still in its infancy but Horner (2002) has identified the following reasons among others for the use of coaching:

- The rate of organisational change. Coaching can provide the space for leaders to identify, reflect on and take action on complex issues.
- Organisational downsizing. Positions that would have prepared managers for more senior positions have been removed so managers have sometimes been promoted faster and lack the necessary leadership skills that coaching can help to build.
- Leadership development has often been reactive and concerned with remedial behavioural change. Coaching can help to pre-empt costly derailment of executives.
- Executive management success is often viewed as a function of the productivity of subordinates. This demands better developed interpersonal and team-building skills which may be assisted by executive coaching.
- It is lonely at the top. In a world where corporate rewards and penalties for success or failure are intense, straightforward counselling within the organisation is often lacking. Coaching can provide a safe and objective haven for executives to develop their ideas.

The essentially human nature of coaching is what makes it work and also what makes it nearly impossible to quantify. Particularly relevant to coaching is the impact of emotional intelligence, covered in Chapter 5, on performance, health and success in work and life. In coaching, as in mentoring, the relationship between the individual and the coach is crucial to success. Coaching will be ineffective if relations between the individual and the coach are ambiguous or because trust between the two is limited. Coaching therefore is likely to work well if the following criteria are met (Bass 1990):

- the individual can identify with the coach and view them as being a good model;
- the coach and individual are open and trusting with each other;
- both accept responsibilities fully;
- the individual is provided with rewards and recognition for improvement.

Coaching can take many forms. Executive coaching focuses on establishing a relationship with individuals that acknowledges and respects their individuality. It is intellectually based on a small number of disciplines including consulting, management, organisational development and psychology. Consequently, executive coaching is the process of equipping people with the tools, knowledge, and opportunities they need to develop themselves and become more effective (Peltier 2001). It helps people to slow down, to find and know themselves better, develop their lives more consciously and to notice the effects of their words and actions on themselves and others. However, coaching does not end with self-awareness. It is a form of action learning that transfers essential communication and relationship skills. Strategic coaching integrates personal development and organisational needs, an approach that can help leaders adapt to new responsibilities, reduce destructive behaviours, enhance teamwork, align individuals to corporate objectives and facilitate and support organisational change. Systematic coaching programmes, reaching whole groups of executives, provide a disciplined way for organisations to deepen relationships with their most important employees and other stakeholders while increasing their effectiveness. The most valuable coaching fosters cultural change for the benefits of the entire organisation. Once senior leaders have changed their behaviour, it is easier for them to influence staff and stakeholders to do the same. At that point change can cascade down an organisational hierarchy (Sherman and Freas 2004).

In the UK a recent guide identified coaching as the fastest-growing training practice in UK business with four-fifths of respondents using coaching and 90 per cent believing that it can improve the bottom-line performance of their organisation (Chartered Institute of Personnel and Development 2004). The coaching organisation, FisherMann, say that their experience of providing executive coaching, mainly in the European public sector, reflects Horner's (ibid.) research, as the following four case studies from their experience exemplify.

1 The newly appointed director

A newly appointed executive director from a predominantly professional background wanted help in handling the politics of his new role, in particular dealing with executive and non-executive aspirations on the governing body of his organisation. His view was that the coaching sessions provided him with the personal space to talk through how these issues were affecting him and what he wanted to do about them. The specific coaching contribution was to encourage him to reach an understanding of his own feelings and aims before helping him to explore what he wanted to do about the issues as he saw them. The outcome, as he described it, was that he had a better understanding of his own management style and was more confident in applying it at board level.

2 The experienced director

An experienced director, having recently taken up post in a new organisation, was finding one of her staff to be extremely difficult to manage, to the point of him being dysfunctional. The director, with the support of her chief executive, sought coaching to try and deal with the member of staff and the problems he was creating. Her first description of the problems she was having was of 'failing and letting her boss down'. The coaching helped her to refocus the issues away from herself to the problems created by her relationship with the staff member and the impact that his actions were having on her team and the performance of the service. The outcome of the coaching sessions was that she no longer felt that the behaviour of someone else was her fault, she was able to develop strategies for dealing with her staff member's performance and behaviour and she, in her own words, felt she could focus on the job to be done rather than focusing on one individual.

3 The ambitious director

A director, who had made several attempts to obtain a more senior post, sought coaching to help her re-think her career development options and to consider alternative ways of achieving fulfilment in her career. The coaching intervention helped her to explore her aspirations in a non-threatening environment and to value her own instincts and feelings rather than trying to mould herself on the perceived wishes of others. The coaching contribution focused on helping the client to recognise for herself the person she wanted to be rather than the person she felt that she should be.

4 The chief executive

An established chief executive wanted to discuss his thoughts and plans for re-focusing and renewing his organisation at a time of significant organisational change. He felt that the organisation expected him to be innovative and visionary, and he was outwardly facing the future with confidence and enthusiasm. Inwardly however, he was questioning whether his ideas were sufficiently progressive. He did not want to be seen as a steady state leader and was conscious that the organisation was ready for change. The coaching sessions gave him the chance, in a confidential setting, to discuss his feelings and thoughts and to renew his purpose in taking the organisation forward. In the case of this particular client the outcome was to strengthen his resolve for his original aim but in other cases it might equally have been to enable him to arrive at the conclusion that it was better for him to move on to something different. This case study emphasises that the coaching purpose is to help the client to arrive at their own conclusions about what they want to do. Usually they can then decide for themselves how to do it.

The common theme through all these case studies is that coaching is very much focused on the individual, their feelings about issues and their personal situation. The coaching is aimed at enabling that person to discover for themselves meanings and solutions to the issues that are often completely unique to them. In that context, it is hard to think of another form of personal development that deliberately does not seek to import other solutions and remedies proven to have worked but which may be totally unacceptable or unworkable for that particular person in his or her own personal circumstances.

COACHING DIFFICULT PEOPLE

We will sometimes encounter or see people with strong personalities who are not happy unless they are at the top of their profession or organisation. These are often referred to as alpha males (Ludeman and Erlandson 2004). The reason these individuals are likely to need executive coaches is because their strengths are also what makes them challenging and frustrating to work with. They tend to be independent and action orientated, taking very high levels of performance for granted, both in themselves and others. The risk is that when alpha males are under pressure to perform, leadership may shift from constructive and challenging to intimidating and possibly abusive. Importantly, these individuals tend to be unemotional and analytical in their approach, preferring to learn about business- and technology-related issues. They have little or no natural curiosity about people or feelings. Consequently, the organisation or service can become dysfunctional because others will often avoid dealing with a difficult alpha male and instead work around or go through the motions of agreeing with him for the sake of maintaining peace and harmony. The approach to coaching people with difficult interpersonal problems is probably best done with 360° feedback analysis. This means taking confidential views from colleagues and other stakeholders who have experience of working with the individual, which is mainly achieved via a structured questionnaire completed anonymously. Once the information from that process has been obtained and analysed then it offers the basis for coaching.

Although there are plenty of successful female leaders with equally strong personalities, they rarely if ever match the complete alpha profile of people who reach the top. In their work with senior executives Ludeman and Erlandson (ibid.) have encountered many women who possess some of the traits of the alpha male but none who possess all of them. Women can be just as data-driven and opinionated and can cope with stress equally well. In that regard it is no surprise that some senior women leaders can be just as challenging to coach as alpha males. Both have achieved success with their particular styles, which makes it difficult for them to see the need for change. However, as we have seen from Chapter 5 on emotional intelligence, the vast majority of women place more value on interpersonal relationships and pay closer attention to the feelings of others. Women more readily understand the importance of positive motivation and the limitations of fear-driven cultures, and so they are less likely to avoid interpersonal issues. Although women leaders are generally comfortable with control and being in charge they tend not to seek to dominate people and situations. Women tend to be less comfortable with conflict, being less willing to force an issue publicly and more interested in collaborating and finding win-win solutions. They will often rise to positions of authority by excelling at collaboration and they are less inclined to resort to intimidation to achieve their objectives. Because women can successfully lead indirectly through relationships and emotions, they run the risk of being accused of being political in style and having hidden agendas because this indirect style can engender distrust among certain kinds of men. Consequently, what women leaders would call diplomacy, some men would tend to call politics.

CONCLUSION

The risk of failure is ever present for all those in leadership positions, whether responsible for an organisation, service or network spanning several organisations. Although there is considerable literature on failure and turning around failing services and organisations, can the literature be distilled into personal leadership behaviours to be applied to minimise the risk of failure? Really good leaders will understand about failure and will increase the probability of success by choosing to work with really good people who are confident in themselves and their own success. In other words, they do not allow their ego to get in the way of what has to be achieved for their organisations or service (Collins 2001).

They are known for their personal humility and a preferred approach of surrounding themselves with individuals whose personal skills and experience complement their own. Not all leaders are able to achieve such a high level of self-confidence straightaway and often it arises as a result of the leader's own developing maturity, wisdom and personal leadership experience. Achieving high levels of self-confidence, which really means confidence in the ability of others (Kanter ibid.), requires not only experience as a leader but also reflective-based personal development that focuses on analysing each leadership experience whether good or bad. A useful starting point for developing a consistently effective leadership approach is to concentrate on the themes presented in this chapter as key pointers for minimising the risk of failure and maximising the probability of personal leadership success. There are eight interdependent personal behaviours that will contribute to personal success, as follows:

1   Be interested in people
     First and foremost, ensure you have a deep and genuine interest in people.
     You must be able to judge individuals, lead teams, grow and coach people,
     be ruthless when required to ensure team focus and harmony, and avoid
     undue favouritism.

2   Be visible
     Be a visible role model. For example if you are asking for more consumer
     focus by your organisation or service but not spending a lot of time with
     consumers yourself, then you are not reflecting your own values and the
     expected behaviour of those around you.

3   Follow through
     Follow through your actions and objectives. Failure to check progress and
     results means leaders are not viewed seriously. Leadership is about delivery
     and failure to follow through agreed objectives can increase the risk of
     failure. It is important in agreeing objectives for both groups and individ-
     uals that you are clearly understood by people in terms of what has to be
     achieved by whom and by when.

4   Stay involved
     Be personally involved in working change through with people. Experi-
     enced leaders know that the possible consequences of change are fairly
     predictable: high levels of perceived inconsistency of personal behaviour
     and results, widespread levels of emotional stress, increasing conflict
     especially within and between groups, and the valuing of past patterns of

behaviour. In spite of these risks being known, many leaders simply do not want to make enough effort to win the hearts and minds of their staff and other stakeholders. They will see this process as repetitive and boring, often preferring to delegate to their immediate team, limit their personal involvement to the start-up period by making a few announcements and then moving on. The reality is that not spending sufficient time in securing the support of key people increases the risk of failure.

5 Listen

Develop good listening skills. We tend not to think about listening when reflecting on our personal development needs but we know from our personal and professional lives that some people are better listeners than others. An ability to listen actively, which can be demonstrated by asking supplementary questions, receiving information or points of view, is very important. If you are seen to be hearing rather than listening then people will ask themselves not only whether you have really heard what is being said but also if you have sufficient commitment to the change.

6 Communicate

Be a good communicator. Frequent and honest communication is essential, particularly when bad news has to be given. Also, remember that developing a 'no surprises' culture should work both ways: you need not only to tell people how they are doing but also ask them how they think you are doing as their leader. Be prepared to act on what they tell you even if you do not like what you hear. This will demonstrate personal maturity.

7 Develop a sense of humour

Develop a good sense of humour. Things will go wrong but not everything that does will be of the same order of magnitude and so a sense of perspective is required. Humour can help shift perspective, allowing people to step back from a problem. Used appropriately, humour also can defuse a tense situation and instil confidence in people to manage a situation that they may think is out of control.

8 Develop self-awareness

Developing your self-awareness can help you understand and analyse your leadership experiences and by so doing, enhance your wisdom, maturity and personal leadership skills for the future. The best way to develop your self-awareness and analyse your experiences is to get a mentor or coach.

DISCUSSION QUESTIONS

1   Are you aware of those components of your job that you enjoy less than others and the tactics you use to ensure they get completed?

2   Are you aware of those aspects of your job that are more stressful than others, and therefore may precipitate increased risk of failure, and do you have ways of managing yourself and your job at these times?

3   Have you experienced a personal leadership failure or been part of a team that has experienced failure and understood the reasons and learning arising from that experience?

4   When failure has occurred have you been able to put the experience into perspective and bounce back to your usual self within a few days? If not, do you understand why, and if not, have you sought help from a mentor or coach?

5   Are you able to deal positively with people issues when they arise in a speedy and objective way?

6   If you hold a senior leadership position, do you have a network or other ways for keeping in touch with reality?

7   If you lead a team do you have some people around you who complement your leadership style by being able to do things that you find difficult or cannot do?

8   In the light of your leadership successes and failures, do you think you would benefit from having a mentor or coach to help you reflect on your experience and develop into a more effective leader?

BIBLIOGRAPHY AND FURTHER READING

Alimo-Metcalfe B. and Lawler J. (2001) Leadership development in UK companies at the beginning of the twenty-first century. Lessons for the NHS? *Journal of Management in Medicine* 15(5): 387–404.

Barnes J. (2003) Turning around failing organisations. A literature review. London: Department of Health Social Care Modernisation Branch.

Bass B.M. (1990) *Bass and Stogdill's Handbook of Leadership Theory, Research and Managerial Applications.* New York: The Free Press.

Bennis W.G. and Thomas R.J. (2002) *Geeks and Geezers.* Boston: Harvard Business School Press.

Chartered Institute of Personnel and Development (2004) *Annual Training and Development Survey.* London: CIPD.

Clutterbuck D. and Ragins B.R. (2002) *Mentoring and Diversity. An international perspective.* Oxford: Butterworth-Heinemann.

Collins J. (2001) *Good to Great.* New York: HarperCollins.

Drucker P.F. (2005) Managing yourself. *Harvard Business Review* January, Special Edition: 100–109.

Glanfield P., Bevington J., Anderson-Walker M. and Appleton L. (2004) Getting to the heart of what matters. *In View: The Journal for Senior Leaders in the NHS*: 20–23.

Goddard M., Mannion R. and Smith P.C. (1999) Assessing the performance of NHS Hospital Trusts: the role of 'hard' and 'soft' information. *Health Policy* 48: 119–134.

Goodwin N. (2002) *The Leadership Role of Chief Executives in the English NHS.* Unpublished PhD thesis. Manchester Business School. University of Manchester.

Heifitz R. (2003) *Leadership Without Easy Answers.* Cambridge, MA: Harvard University Press.

Higgins J. (2001) The listening blank. *Health Service Journal* 111: 22–25.

Hirst G., Mann L., Bain P., Pirola-Merlo A. and Richver A. (2004) Learning to lead: the development and testing of a model of leadership learning. *The Leadership Quarterly* 15: 311 – 327.

HM Government (2001) *The Report of the Public Inquiry into Children's Heart Surgery at the Bristol Royal Infirmary 1984–1995: learning from Bristol* (CM 5207 (I)) London: HMSO.

Horner C. (2002) *Executive Coaching: the leadership development tool of the future?* MBA dissertation, Imperial College, London.

Hudson F. (1999) *The Handbook of Coaching.* San Francisco: Jossey-Bass.

Joyce P. (2004) The role of leadership in the turnaround of a local authority. *Public Money and Management* 24(4): 235–242.

Kanter R.M. (2004) *Confidence. How winning streaks and losing streaks begin and end.* London: Random House Business Books.

Kellerman B. (2004) *Bad Leadership: what it is, how it happens, why it matters.* Boston: Harvard Business School Press.

Ludeman K. and Erlandson E. (2004) Coaching the alpha male. *Harvard Business Review* May: 58–67.

Mintzberg H. (2004) *Managers Not MBAs. A hard look at the soft practice of managing and management development.* Harlow, UK: Pearson Education Limited.

Øvretveit J. (2004) *The Leaders Role in Quality and Safety Improvement. A review of research and guidance.* Stockholm: Association of Swedish County Councils (Lanstingsforbundet).

Parslowe E. and Wray M. (2003) *Coaching and Mentoring. Practical methods to improve learning.* London: Kogan Page.

Peltier B. (2001) *The Psychology of Executive Coaching.* London: Brunner-Routledge.

Sherman S. and Freas A. (2004) The wild west of executive coaching. *Harvard Business Review* November: 82–90.

Walsh K., Harvey G., Hyde P. and Pandit N. (2004) Organisational failure and turn-around: lessons for public services from the for-profit sector. *Public Money and Management* 24(4): 201–208.

Walshe K. and Shortell S. (2004) When things go wrong: how health care organisations deal with major failures. *Health Affairs* 23(3): 103–111.

Conclusion

The analysis and approach to leadership presented in this book reflects the strongly contextual aspect of leading health care across Europe. Although no European countries are alike each country is increasingly facing the same significant challenges. What this means above all else is continual change, but delivering that in a transformational and sustainable way will be very challenging and probably for some countries, impossible. The leadership challenge of managing the changes being pursued by most countries of Europe is not to be underestimated, not only for the countries and governments concerned but also for the millions of health care staff that will be affected. Governments are demanding change to the structure and systems of their health care services and the people leadership challenges will be enormous. Leadership is about change and it is about people: it is a dynamic, interpersonal-based process that increasingly has to be practised not only within but also across organisational boundaries. For that reason, the leadership approach that has been presented here focuses on pursuing change based on the development of effective and sustainable interpersonal and inter-organisational relationships, underpinned by the leader committing to a proactive, self-awareness-based approach to personal development driven by analysis of previous leadership experiences.

The leadership approach also has been supported by the presentation of a major qualitative research study into chief executive leadership demonstrating for health care leaders at all levels how leadership can be practised in their day-to-day world. The outcome of that research, coupled with the description of leadership in this book, provides a practical way forward for a leadership-based approach to managing change in public services and health care across Europe. The research was undertaken on the basis that leadership research needs to adopt a more holistic, contextual approach rather than the alternative of focusing on one or two specific organisational or leadership variables, as has frequently been the case in much historical leadership research both generally and in the health care sector (Pettigrew and Whipp 1993; Pettigrew *et al.* 1994; Rost 1993).

In their paper on future challenges for research into organisational change Pettigrew *et al.* (2001) argue that the impact of time, process, discontinuity and context are still insufficiently understood in organisational change. This is exacerbated by the increasing complexity facing not only the commercial sector because of the globalisation of markets, but also European health care because of its political, economic and general operating contexts. A new pluralism of organisational change research is called for, comprising multiple levels of analysis and the reciprocal study of contexts and change actions that take into account time, history and the presentation of change as a continuous process rather than a detached episode.

Pettigrew *et al.* (2001) also emphasise that there remains a dearth of research linking organisational change to organisational performance. A new dimension on linking change and leadership is offered by Wheatley (1999) who discusses moving away from the somewhat traditional engineering-based thinking of organisational change in which problematic organisations are treated as broken machines with the failing parts merely identified and replaced. The alternative approach is to view organisations as systems, which essentially is how European health care increasingly operates. Wheatley argues that although systems are composed of parts they cannot be understood solely by only looking at the parts. It is necessary to work with the whole of a system in order to understand its dynamics at any moment in time, a view derived from quantum physics and chaos theory. These views chime with leadership being viewed as a dynamic, relationship-based intra- and inter-organisational process with a strong emphasis on transformation. Therefore, real change needs to be seen as rooted in personal behaviours or when individuals see change within organisations or across systems that enables them to contribute more to what they have already defined as meaningful in their work. Further, there are links with networks. Although information may energise a network it is the people in the network who decide what is meaningful to them, requiring leaders to pay close attention to interpersonal, intra-organisational and inter-organisational processes.

A greater understanding of the issues arising from the above may help answer what is probably the most important leadership question of practical importance to leaders, raised by Pettigrew *et al.* (2001) and arising from the research outcomes presented in Chapter 6, namely what is the relationship between the management of change processes and organisational performance? The research of Goodwin (2002) suggests that leadership is the unique variable that accounts for performance variations within organisations over time, at least within the English NHS and probably for the majority of health care and public service organisations. However, the four health authority case studies also raise issues other than the variables that constituted the basis of the research, namely leadership, inter-organisational relationships and the impact of the unique features of the environment for public services. The other issues raised by the case studies include power relationships, perceptions of organisational performance and organisational success, and specific attributes of inter-organisational networking such as trust and the management of negative, rather than positive, networks. These and related issues need to constitute the core of the organisational research agenda of the future and they can probably be distilled into the following five research questions:

1   Is there a relationship between organisational change, organisational performance and leadership?
2   Can future research move away from the increasingly anachronistic question, does leadership matter, to the more important question, under what conditions and context can leadership make a difference?
3   What future contributions can the network and networking literature make to defining and explaining leadership?
4   Can a more holistic approach to leadership research be pursued linking leadership to other literature such as trust and power?
5   Can the impact of the environment be researched from the perspective of inter-organisational collaboration rather than the traditional and historical single organisation based approach?

This research agenda offers enormous potential to make a significant contribution to leadership research. However, researchers have been chided for not bridging the gap between theoretical knowledge and its practical application (Pettigrew *et al.* 2001; Rost 1993). To bridge the gap requires not only exploring change processes through time and context but also engaging much more with actual management practice. One way forward would be to encourage individuals to work across both research and practice adopting a partnership approach to the funding, production and dissemination of future research.

Finally, there are implications for selecting and developing health care leaders flowing from the approach to leadership presented in this book, the strong operating context of Europe's health care services and from the research results presented in Chapter 6. To recap, the conclusion of the research is that where health care leadership does exist it is rooted in the successful tackling of significant local issues based on an approach of developing effective networking and interpersonal skills and inter-organisational relationships. In turn, this approach is most likely to drive the local implementation of bigger, nationally driven strategies for change. Consequently, developing health care leaders need to focus on personal learning and reflection based on their experience of tackling significant local challenges. The implications for selecting and developing the health care leaders of the future are fourfold.

First, the selection of senior health care executives, especially those aspiring to chief executive posts, needs to include assessment of their ability to form effective interpersonal relationships and by so doing, being able to influence other organisations through the development of inter-organisational networks. For the reasons given in Chapter 5, the selection process should include an emotional intelligence-based component approach because of the greater impact of emotional intelligence at the top of organisations on corporate and personal success.

Second, because not only the context of each countries' health care system is different but also the context of local health care systems within each country, leadership is best learned and developed through the successful tackling of significant local issues. Governments should exercise restraint in the setting of national targets and criteria in order for local chief executives, managers and clinical leaders to have optimum freedom to develop a local leadership culture. This would not only increase the probability of sustainable rather than short-term results being produced but also develop a foundation of strong and effective interpersonal and inter-organisational relationships for when local health care leaders are required to implement nationally or regionally driven change.

Third, the extent to which leadership can be learned via participation in classroom-based development programmes is limited. National and regional governments can best support leadership development by providing the necessary resources and personal and organisational development support for local consumption. If national or regional resources are used to support such an approach then their use can be assessed within a national or regional leadership development framework that outlines senior and corporate leadership requirements for all health care organisations.

Fourth, given the increasingly multi-sectoral and inter-agency approach to health and health care management, much greater emphasis needs to be given to learning how to develop inter-organisational networks and influencing both within and beyond health care organisations. Inter-organisational rather than intra-organisational development practitioners need to be available to support local health care leaders if they are to be more successful in working across inter-organisational, inter-sectoral and inter-agency boundaries.

BIBLIOGRAPHY AND FURTHER READING

Goodwin N. (2002) *Determining the Leadership Role of Chief Executives in the English NHS*. Unpublished PhD thesis. Manchester Business School, University of Manchester.

Pettigrew A. and Whipp R. (1993) *Managing Change for Competitive Success*. Oxford: Blackwell.

Pettigrew A., Ferlie E. and McKee L. (1994) *Shaping Strategic Change, Making Change in Large Organisations: the case of the National Health Service*. London: Sage.

Pettigrew A., Woodman R.W. and Cameron K.M. (2001) Studying organizational change and development: challenges for future research. *Academy of Management Journal* 44(4): 697–713.

Rost J.C. (1993) *Leadership for the Twenty-First Century*. London: Praeger.

Wheatley M.J. (1999) *Leadership and the New Science. Discovering order in a chaotic world*. San Francisco: Berrett-Koehler.

Index

185